SHARED THREADS

To Carolyn

Shared quilt

Crazy Mary S-

1. A few of the 20,064 panels comprising the AIDS Memorial Quilt that were displayed on The Mall in Washington, D.C., October 1992 (see also fig. 144, pages 128-129 in the Epilogue). Photograph by Mark Thiessen courtesy The NAMES Project, San Francisco, California.

SHARED THREADS

Quilting Together—Past and Present

Jacqueline Marx Atkins

in association with
Museum of American Folk Art
New York

Dedicated to the memory of
Robert Bishop,
friend, mentor, and ongoing source of inspiration,
and to the memory of
Edna Brayton,
whose love of and skill in quilting was matched by her
generous nature and ability to share

VIKING STUDIO BOOKS

Published by the Penguin Group
Penguin Books USA Inc., 375 Hudson Street,
New York, New York, 10014, U.S.A.

Penguin Books Ltd, 27 Wrights Lane,
London W8 5TZ, England

Penguin Books Australia Ltd, Ringwood,
Victoria, Australia

Penguin Books Canada Ltd, 2801 John Street,
Markham, Ontario, Canada L3R 1B4

Penguin Books (N.Z.) Ltd, 182-90 Wairau Road,
Auckland 10, New Zeland

Penguin Books Ltd, Registered Offices:
Harmondsworth, Middlesex, England

First published by Viking Studio Books, an imprint of Penguin Books USA Inc.

First printing, June, 1994
10 9 8 7 6 5 4 3 2 1

Library of Congress
Catalog Card Number: 94-60097

Book designed by Marilyn Rey
Printed and bound by Dai Nippon Printing Co., Hong Kong, Ltd.

ISBN: 0-525-93441-3 (cloth); ISBN: 0-525-48603-8 (paperback)

Contents

Acknowledgments

Just as the quilts shown in this book drew on the talents and skills of many makers, so too did the creation of the book itself rely on input from a widespread network of people. *Shared Threads* pulls together many of the myriad bits of information on group quilting that have appeared in a variety of sources over the years, and my sincere thanks and appreciation are due to all those whose careful research and diligent work I have drawn on in putting this book together. Many, many people have also given generously of their time and energy in providing me with needed information and in helping me track down more obscure bits of data; many others provided ongoing support in both tangible and intangible ways, and I would like to make special note of several of them here. Phyllis A. Tepper, Director of the New York Quilt Project, Museum of American Folk Art, New York City, was outstanding in her support and help in the course of my work on this book. Joan Bloom and Deborah Ash, students and interns in the Folk Art Institute, Museum of American Folk Art, provided much-welcomed and necessary help in fact-checking, locating images, and clearing permissions, and I am indebted to Barbara Cate and Lee Kogan, respectively Director and Associate Director of the Institute, for making the interns available to assist me. My thanks also to Bob Bishop and Gerard Wertkin, former and present Directors of the Museum of American Folk Art, for their support of this project, and to other staff of the Museum who provided assistance. Caroline Kerrigan, a Museum interne working under the supervision of Cathy Rasmussen, also provided invaluable background research for the sections on political, patriotic, and public quilts.

Curators, quilt makers, quilt owners, quilt historians, quilt dealers, and many others have patiently answered my questions, helped to locate material, and generously shared their time and knowledge to facilitate my work on this book, among them: ABC Quilts, Brooklyn, New York, especially Donna Boyle, Maureen McCormack, and Angie Roth; Boise Peace Quilt Project, Boise, Idaho, especially Heidi Read; Ruthanne Brod, New York State Museum, Albany, New York; Bennett Carlson, The NAMES Project, San Francisco, California; Sue C. Cummings, Ph.D.; Marcia Eymann and Inez Brooks-Meyers, The Oakland Museum, Oakland, California; Pat Ferrero, Hearts and Hands Media Arts, San Francisco, California; Laura Fisher/Antique Quilts and Americana, New York City; Louise Francke; Marjorie Freund; Victoria Hoffman; Marilynn Karp; Kei Kobayashi; Joel and Kate Kopp, America Hurrah Antiques, New York City; Celia LoPinto, California Heritage Quilt Project, San Francisco, California; Patricia Mears, The Brooklyn Museum, Brooklyn, New York; Judith and James Milne, Inc., New York City; Paula Nadelstern; Mary H. Nash; Laurel Nilsen, Lynn Historical Society, Lynn, Massachusetts; Susan Parrish, New York City; Bets Ramsey; Cindy Rennels, Cindy's Quilts, Clinton, Oklahoma; Daniel B. Reibel, Old Barracks Museum, Trenton, New Jersey; Teresa Roane, Valentine Museum, Richmond, Virginia; Diane Schneck; Doris Shandell; Susan Shie; Mrs. Walter E. Simmons II; Aurelie Stack; Wilma Townsend, Ontario County Historical Society, Canandaigua, New York; Gail Treschel, Birmingham Museum of Art, Birmingham, Alabama; Nancy Tuckhorn, Daughters of the American Revolution Museum, Washington, D.C.; Michael Vitucci, WCTU; Merikay Waldvogel; Gail Doering Weimer, Oneida Community Mansion House, Oneida, New York; and Bob Wilson, Metro New York Quilters, New York City. Shelly Zegart, Louisville, Kentucky, has my ever-lasting appreciation for the information she provided about the Young Ladies Sewing Society of Canandaigua and their quilts, as well as for offering me a friendly sounding board at times of frustration.

Special thanks are also due to Karen Bell and Scott Bowron for their careful and skillful photography of many of the quilts in this book.

And not least, my sincere thanks to my editor, Cyril I. Nelson, for his belief in this book and his willingness to bring it to fruition, and to my husband, Edward G. Atkins, for his ongoing patience, support, and encouragement.

Foreword

When the author asked me to write this foreword I was pleased for more than one reason. Her contributions to the literature of quiltmaking history have established her as a serious and accurate recorder of that history. We had been collaborators on *New York Beauties: Quilts from the Empire State*. Her talents as a writer and the insights she offered into the enormous amount of material we were faced with made a difficult task surmountable.

Shared Threads: Quilting Together Past and Present celebrates the relationships fostered through shared activity. It goes beyond the conventional approach to group quilting that has appeared in numerous books and magazine articles over the past several years by pulling together myriad bits of information and placing them within a social and cultural context. Atkins expands on the definition of group-made quilts and pushes the boundaries beyond those previously accepted; for example, changing technology has made it possible for participants to interact by computer to create a quilt.

The author provides the history and reasons for the way this unique American textile tradition has progressed through the years from a need to exchange labor in a frontier society to its contemporary emphasis on social cooperation among diverse participants. Along the way she demythologizes the romantic notion of quilting by commenting on the communal nature of American society as a continuum; that the dynamics of social and economic changes affect the reasons why people come together although the underlying needs for human interaction remain the same. She reflects on the changing role of women and how the use of the needle (that peculiar skill designated as "women's work") has changed with the times. The book reminds us of the social contract, historically the basis for America's essence, that of shared and reciprocal rights and duties within a cultural context. It is rich in traditional lore about customs and rituals assigned to communal quilt making and provides an understanding of the continuum of change and metamorphosis into such new forms as an international wedding quilt.

The main types of quilts discussed include friendship quilts, family quilts, wedding quilts, mourning quilts, fundraising quilts, presentation and commemorative quilts, quilts for social causes (AIDS quilt, WCTU quilts), peace quilts, patriotic quilts, and quilts for the fun of making quilts.

The book is inclusive of quiltmakers long neglected in the quilt-history literature, such as slave women and women working in quilt cottage industries to supplement earnings. By illuminating this special activity of women this book adds not only to quilt history but to women's history as well. During the process of writing *New York Beauties* we were struck with the numbers of quilts made by more than one person, the motivations for the making of those quilts, the social context, and the effects of that social conditioning. I am pleased that this book contains a few of the quilts documented by the New York Quilt Project that were not included in *New York Beauties* because of publishing constraints.

PHYLLIS A. TEPPER

2. Friendship Album; makers from New York and New Jersey; New York environs; 1851–1853; pieced and appliquéd cotton; 85½″ x 73″. (New Jersey State Museum Collection, CH1987.38. Trenton, New Jersey.) This quilt combines a medley of popular elements of the time, from patriotic symbols, to classic signature blocks, to favored patterns, but it was probably made as a wedding present, if the inscription of "Best Wishes" on one block can be taken to give an indication of intent. Some of the signatures were clearly relatives of the unknown recipient ("Aunt Lydia Higgins," "Your Grandmother/Lydia Dey/Brooklyn 1851"); others seem to be members of the same or related families. A number of men signed the quilt, but it is most likely that the women of their families made the blocks that they signed, a not uncommon event of the time.

The Tie that Binds

"The plough is hardly a more blessed instrument in America than the needle."[1]

"History chronicles the large and glorious deeds of the standard bearers...and tell[s] nothing at all of the courageous women who keep the business of the house going. The world has never seen such hardihood, such perseverance, such devotion, nor such ingenuity in making the best of everything as was displayed by America's pioneer women. Their like has never been known."[2]

Throughout the years of women's history, sewing has, in many ways, been the shared thread that has tied women together. Of all the skills associated most closely with women, sewing is the common denominator—the one that has had the ability to cut across barriers of class, education, social and economic position, ethnicity, and religious beliefs. For much of the period of documented and undocumented history, it has been a skill of crucial domestic importance, functionally necessary to the well-being of a family, yet one that by its very nature encouraged the expression of creativity as well as the joys of both solitary and shared accomplishment. It is a thread that has, over the years, bound untold numbers of women together through common chores and mutual needs and beliefs. Although its importance in daily life today is significantly diminished, it still retains the ability to draw women together for both work and companionship, for the sharing of common goals, and for the establishment of ongoing bonds.

Sewing is often an individual and solitary activity, but there has always been a strong social component to it. There are more references to sewing in early diaries than to almost any other woman's task, and many of these entries also refer to women working together and to quilting—an activity that lends itself well to communal work.[3] Of all the elements on which women have lavished their considerable needlework skill through the years, perhaps nowhere is the mutuality of relationships between and among them more evident than in quilting. Quilts have long played an important role in the textile tradition of this country—functionally, as a means of providing warmth; culturally, as expressions of the lives, beliefs, and history of the women who made them; and socially, as a means for women to gather and work together in friendship, solidarity, and mutual aid.

During the Colonial period, until near the end of the eighteenth century, homes in America, particularly those in rural areas, were often far apart, transportation was limited, tasks related to basic survival sometimes seemed unending, and opportunities for friendly interchange were frequently restricted. Although much work was carried out on a reciprocal basis within the extended family unit itself, larger communal work parties, or

3. Sampler; makers unknown; northeastern United States; c. 1905; pieced and appliquéd cotton; size not available. Photograph courtesy of Laura Fisher/Antique Quilts and Americana, New York City. (Private collection) The blocks in this sampler quilt carry signatures that appear to be members of several different families, possibly related by marriage. Although no information is known about the quilt, it is a good example of its genre and was probably made as a token of friendship or possibly as a bridal gift. Given the clinging popularity of Crazy quilts at the time, it is interesting to find a reversion to a style more popular at mid-century.

4. Chintz Album Counterpane; makers unknown; southern United States; mid-nineteenth century; appliquéd cotton; 112″ x 109″. Photograph by Ken Burris. (Collection of Shelburne Museum, Shelburne, Vermont) The lovely chintz blocks in this piece were apparently collected from family members over several years and then joined together by one person. The inscriptions read "To Mother 1854," "Mother from Sue 1855," "Sister Polly from Mary," "Mother from Connie 1855," "Mother from Pattie," and "To my cousin Mary from R.I.W. 1850." The quilt was passed down through a New England family, but it had never been used because it had been stolen from a Southern home during the Civil War, and the Yankee family was ashamed of the theft.

"bees" as they were often called, served a crucial role in meeting both the subsistence and social needs of Colonial and pioneer life, for work and sociable intercourse often went hand-in-hand in that preindustrial period.[4] Comments from chroniclers of these times make clear the shared work aspect as well as the social aspect of these gatherings:

> Raisings, logging bees, husking bees, quilting bees, and the many other occasions in which the word bee was used to indicate the gathering of the settlers to render gratuitous aids to some neighbor in need... was merely the voluntary union of the individual aid and strength of an entire community to assist a settler in doing what he was unable to accomplish alone. Hence by bees the pioneers raised their houses and barns, did their logging, husked their corn, quilted their bed coverings, and enjoyed themselves in frolic and song with the girls in the evening.[5]

Of as much importance as the work accomplished at these gatherings was the opportunity to meet with friends and new neighbors (and perhaps prospective partners) and to share food, conversation, and some lighthearted play after the main work of the day was done. The events not only met the need for helping hands and companionship, invitations to them were also a sign of acceptance in the community. As one early recorder put it:

> A failure to ask a neighbour to a raising, clearing, chopping frolic, or his family to a quilting, was considered a high indignity.... Each settler was not only willing but desirous to contribute his share to the general comfort and public improvement, and felt aggrieved and insulted if the opportunity to do so were withheld.[6]

Thus, neighbors helping neighbors was the norm rather than the exception, and help was given when and where needed in the secure knowledge that reciprocity was the order of the day.

With almost all chores, whether large-scale or small, help was welcomed and enjoyed both for the relief provided and for the companionship that accompanied it; socialization may have been a secondary aspect to the work accomplished, but no less important for all that. Sewing and quilting, whether on clothes or bedding, was an area in which work was regularly exchanged by women, both on a family and a neighborly level, and was a logical extension of the Colonial practices of "change-work" and "the whang," terms for work in which housewives helped each other with tasks in alteration or gathered together in small groups at one another's homes to speed a large job like spring cleaning.[7] Sewing was also an activity that did not hinge on the vagaries of weather, and something could always be accomplished, whether the time devoted to it was an hour or a day. It also allowed women a time together to strengthen bonds and share feelings.

As life was reshaped in the nineteenth century, exchange labor and mutual aid was still an integral part of working together, but it was far less crucial to daily survival than in earlier years. Cooperative work among men began to wane as the country shifted from a frontier dynamic to more established modes of life. The *Farmer's Almanack* claimed such work was inefficient and wasteful; it was viewed "more for the sport than to do any real good."[8] House and barn raisings, however, remained in favor (especially in frontier and rural areas) as they still required more labor and skills than one man could effectively and rapidly supply, but most other work rituals shared by males were in decline as early as 1825. Even though much of the country remained tied to a rural/agricultural mode of life, the growth of an urban population, a move to a market economy, an increase in personal wealth that allowed employing help rather than buying it with "affectionate regard," specialization of tasks, advances in technology, and a gradually decreasing frontier—all played a part in lessening the need for communal labor. Men still worked together for the common good when necessary, especially in rural areas, but these occasions were now more likely to be acts of charity—a "wood bee," for example, would be held to provide fuel for an indigent family—and recognized as such rather than as part of the normal way to get things done.[9]

Traditional forms of women's communal work also began to change focus at about this time as the concept of "woman's sphere" developed and became firmly entrenched, at least in the middle and upper classes of society.[10] As men's work options were expanding, women's contracted. A woman's sphere of influence became relegated more and more to home, hearth, and family; men held the dominant position in almost all other endeavors.[11] A part of this new view also idealized women as being more sensitive than men, with a perceived purer nature and greater moral strength; it was thus seen as part of a woman's duty to improve the outside world as well as her home. Much of this perception of women fit well with the growth of the romantic ideal of friendship, the seeds of which had been sown toward the end of the eighteenth century. This paradigm continued well into the nineteenth century, bringing with it the full flowering of the friendship concept in autograph albums and Friendship quilts. Ironically, the concept of "woman's sphere" served to push women even more closely together, excluding men as it did from so many of the basic functions of everyday life and emphasizing the bonds between women.

As the real need for exchange labor among women decreased for many of the same reasons as it did with men (although market economy never played a role, as the

5. Chimney Sweep Album; Adah Bingham McKelvey and others; Roanerville area, California; 1870–1880; pieced cotton; 93″ x 81″. Photograph by Sharon Risedorph courtesy California Heritage Quilt Project. (Collection of Webb McKelvey) The family name for this quilt is "The John Brown Quilt" because it was made at a quilting party given in honor of the abolitionist's widow. John Brown was hanged as a traitor for his raid on the federal arsenal at Harper's Ferry, Virginia, in 1859. Mary Ann Brown, his widow and second wife, then left her New York home with four of his twenty children and made the difficult overland trek to California, arriving "a hungry, almost barefoot, ragged lot," as reported in the *San Francisco Chronicle*. Mrs. Brown worked as a midwife, and two of her daughters taught black children (although legislation following the Civil War allowed blacks to attend public schools, in reality they were hardly made welcome), but her life remained difficult. Adah McKelvey, the wife of a Methodist minister who built churches in many parts of California, heard of Mrs. Brown while the McKelvey family were living nearby, and she arranged a quilting party where Mrs. Brown and her daughters were the guests of honor. All the women in attendance were supportive of the widow, and each signed her name to this quilt. Mrs. Brown and her daughters Ellen and Sadie signed, respectively, the last block on the right in the next to bottom row, the block immediately to its left, and the center block in the fourth row from the top.

6. Counterpane; said to have been made by British sailors; New York environs; early nineteenth century; pieced, appliquéd, and embroidered wool; 94⅝″ x 80⅝″. (Collection of The Smithsonian Institution, Washington, D.C.) This counterpane has an intriguing oral history. It is said to have been created by sailors on a British sailing vessel and given to a Mr. Graf, the owner of a tavern on the New York waterfront, as payment for money owed to him by the sailors. The red fabric is thought to have come from the uniforms of British soldiers of the War of 1812; the other fabrics are sturdy wool that would have served hard-working men well.

7. Friendship Album; Sewing Society of the Methodist Episcopal Church; Elizabethport, New Jersey; 1852; appliquéd cotton; 99¼″ x 100″. (Collection of Museum of American Folk Art, New York City; Gift of Phyllis Haders. 1980.1.1.) This presentation quilt was made by the Society for the Reverend and Mrs. Dunn, missionaries and lay preachers to islands in the South Pacific. The church shown on the block in the third row is most likely a representation of the Elizabethport Methodist Episcopal Church as it was when the quilt was made. Two similar presentation quilts are known, one now at the American Museum in Britain (Bath, England), and the other at the Newark Museum, Newark, New Jersey. Similar or identical blocks appear on the quilts (see detail), and many of the signatures are the same, indicating that the makers were a close-knit group with similar interests, even though they may have belonged to different churches (research has connected the two other quilts, respectively, to the First Baptist Church and the First Presbyterian Church, both within a mile or so of the Methodist Episcopal Church). Many blocks in all three quilts contain religious symbolism and sayings. (For more information, see Lee Kogan, "The Quilt Legacy of Elizabeth, New Jersey," *The Clarion*, Winter 1990, pp. 58–64.)

8. Detail—This unusual printed fabric (see next to bottom row of quilt in figure 7, page 5) also appears on the quilt owned by the American Museum in Britain and was a major clue in linking the two pieces. (Photograph by Lee Kogan)

THE FAIRY SEWING-MACHINE. A HOLIDAY GIFT FOR THE WORK-TABLE

9. An advertisement for "The Fairy Sewing Machine," a tiny forerunner that helped speed up certain sewing chores and was portable enough to allow women to carry it with them and work with their friends. The advent of the full-size sewing machine, with its much greater capacity, quickly made this invention obsolete. Courtesy The Smithsonian Institution, Washington, D.C.

10. Detail—White Whole Cloth; Mrs. A.J. Lewis and Miss Harriet L. Jones; location unknown; 1870; cotton; size unavailable. (Courtesy The Oakland Museum History Department, Acc. # H23.2303, Oakland, California) When the sewing machine became available in the early 1850s, *Godey's Lady's Book* referred to it as "The Queen of Inventions," and women embraced this new technology with all the fervor sometimes attributed to religion. The rapidity of the sewing-machine's acceptance is underscored in this entry in *Moore's Rural New-Yorker* (September 23, 1854): "About five years ago we do not believe there were more than three or four sewing machines in use in our country; now they can be counted by the thousands." The high regard that some women felt for their machines can be seen in this quilt made by two women who paid the machine they used the highest compliment— they stitched the model name, the American Com. Machine, along with their names right into the quilt. The machine was apparently the property of Mrs. Ada Jones (possibly Harriet's mother), whose name also appears on the quilt. It was not unusual in those early days for women to share their machines and teach each other their new skills.

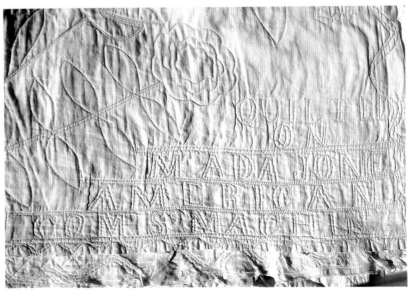

concept of "woman's sphere" placed a low premium on the value of women's work), the social importance of the women's work gatherings of earlier times decreased, too, especially as urban dwellers found more arenas for social intercourse open to them. More consciously purposeful and organized forms of activity began to compete with the less formal gatherings of earlier years as the concept of quilting for causes, for "doing good," made itself felt. Church-related women's benevolent groups based on the traditional cooperative and exchange work concept developed, largely as a result of the Second Great Awakening, but partly also as a result of what was considered to be appropriately a part of women's sphere—caring for the needs of the community as well as the home. Thus, women continued to do needlework together, but there was now an overt philanthropic overlay that cast such work within the context of benefit for the larger community—be it local or national in scale—rather than for the benefit of friends, family, and neighbors.[12] Although family members and close neighbors still worked together on occasion, by the end of the nineteenth century group quilting was almost invariably a tightly structured and organized women-only affair, often church- or grange-related, and usually held with some larger social or humanitarian purpose in mind—be it fundraising, providing goods for the needy, or making a presentation gift for a worthy community member.

As the twentieth century opened, the concept of "woman's sphere" essentially disappeared, leaving as its legacy the depreciation of the women's skills it had engendered; those such as needlework that had once proved so fundamental and invaluable a part of everyday life now had virtually no value. A "culture of consumption" began to take effect, as the Industrial Revolution reached its maturity and technological advances allowed the purchase of more and more items that once required hours of production in the home.[13]

Quilting, whether done alone or with others, began an almost inevitable decline. Although it never completely disappeared, as can be seen by the many newspaper columns devoted to quilt patterns and the many fundraising quilts that continued to be made, quilting seemed to be relegated primarily to rural and poor areas, where it remained in some cases a necessity and in others part of a benevolent effort with sociable overtones. A brief resurgence occurred during World War I as women throughout the country joined together to make Red Cross quilts, and again during the Great Depression, when economic hardship forced many, of necessity, to return to the skills of their mothers and grandmothers. Although women continued to quilt together throughout this period, and socialization remained an important element, the communal quilting frolics as revered in literature were but a distant memory.

The 1940s and 1950s were perhaps the low point in quilt history, as first World War II and then a growing economy brought about even more dramatic changes in life style. Communal quilting was no longer a significant part of life, either in the city or the country; as one rural woman sadly noted, recalling earlier years: "We had more time to visit and there was some social life. But today neighbors never go, it seems, back and forth....I know that we as neighbors used to gather in and we'd quilt or something, you know, and have a big dinner 'n things, which we don't do anymore....And it seems as though today, no, they don't neighbor back at all and forth."[14] Women not only had found other means of socializing; they were also becoming part of the work force in ever-growing numbers and abandoning the skills of their predecessors in favor of the new skills of the technological age.

By the 1960s, few women retained much knowledge of the nineteenth-century craft tradition that had once empowered them, and when the quilting revival of the 1970s began, many women found it necessary to regain those skills, often through revival of yet another old tradition—working together. Today, women are free to sew by choice rather than by necessity, and the bonds of friendship that are established and reinforced through group projects are often more important than the work carried out.

Quilting still holds the promise of friendship, creativity, and exchange. Many women today gather together to quilt in part to negate some of the anomie and alienation that the rush of modern life has promoted; the energy of pooled efforts strengthens each, and the bonds grow. Yet, the intrinsic urge to work together—whether the end result is for one person's benefit as in a spectacular wedding quilt made by a group of friends, or for a common cause as in the panels of the AIDS Memorial Quilt made by women, men, and children who may know each other only through their stitchery—has not died out, but only shows a greater strength as participants come together in both traditional and innovative ways to satisfy that urge to touch, exchange, and share.

11. Bull's Eye; inmates at the Women's State Prison; West Nashville, Davidson County, Tennessee; c. 1933; pieced cotton; 74″ x 71″. Photograph courtesy Merikay Waldvogel. (Collection of Kay Hardy) Quilting together could provide both a means of socialization and a way to pass the time that might otherwise lie heavily on a prisoner; it might also help a woman cut off from family and friends to retain some ties to the activities of her former life. Eula Erwin, matron and, along with her husband, caretaker at the women's prison in West Nashville, encouraged the inmates to occupy themselves with quilting, gardening, and cooking. She sometimes provided scraps from worn-out inmate uniforms for quilting, but also often bought new materials for the inmates to use. This quilt might have been inspired by the Nancy Page column in the *Nashville Banner* of May 9, 1933, which featured the Bull's Eye pattern. The present owner of the quilt is the niece of Mrs. Erwin.

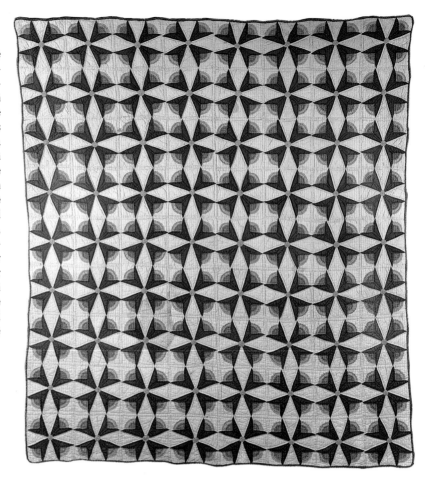

12. Eula and Buford Erwin, standing, with staff and some of the fifty inmates of the Women's Prison near Nashville, 1933. Photograph courtesy Merikay Waldvogel.

13. Hatfield-McCoy Victory Quilt; America Hatfield McCoy, Rhoda McCoy, and other family members; Kentucky; 1943; pieced and appliquéd cotton; 78″ x 94″. Photograph courtesy Kentucky Historical Society, Frankfort, Kentucky. (Collection of Ohio Historical Society, Columbus, Ohio) The Hatfields of West Virginia and the McCoys of Kentucky are well known in American lore for their long-standing feud, which had its roots in the Civil War and which was the cause of at least six murders. This quilt was made by two women (one of them a Hatfield) who married McCoy brothers; they were helped by women from both families, and the quilt symbolizes the end of the feud. Rhoda McCoy inscribed most of the names in pencil on the quilt (America could neither read nor write), and women of the families then stitched those as well as names of other kinsmen into the quilt. The quilt also clearly expresses the patriotism of the times, as underlined in this ballad, written to commemorate the making of the quilt.

I've been down to the quiltin'
folks,
A victory quilt they say;
At Granny Hatfield's old log
house
Across on Tadpole Way.

And Rhoda, Bud McCoy's
good wife
With Martha Hatfield, too,
Made up the quilt of calico
With old red, white and blue.

One big star stands for Devil
Anse,
Who led the Rebel Clan,
Another star—Harmon
McCoy
A faithful Union Man.

Woodrow McCoy, another
star,
For many victories won,
He was a proud and noble
lad,
America Hatfield's son.

The last big star, a Hatfield
boy,
Old Tolbert's pride was he,
The small stars, Ace and
Anderson
Who fought across the sea.

This victory quilt to honor
them
We'll place within a shrine
With Roosevelt's name and
noble deeds
On history's page to shine.

14. Quilt-guild members work together to complete a quilt destined for local humanitarian use.

15. *Ozark Quilting Bee*; "Grandma Fran" (Frances Currey Brown); watercolor; 1985. (Courtesy the artist and Rogers Historical Museum, Rogers, Arkansas)

Many Hands Make Light Work

"The quilting is mostly a feminine arrangement. Its ostensible object is the manufacture of a bedquilt. This involved a social gathering—talk, tea, probably a little gossip and scandal, and in the evening the accession of masculinity, with more or less of fun and frolic."[1]

"The ladies of the Union are great workers, and among other enterprises of ingenious industry, they frequently fabricate patchwork quilts. When the external composition of one of these is complete, it is usual to call together their neighbors and friends to witness, and assist at the quilting, which is the completion of this elaborate work. These assemblings are called 'quilting frolics,' and they are always solemnised with much good cheer and festivity."[2]

"I went to Mrs. Low's quilting. There was 15 to quilt   had 2 quilts and there was indeed meery faces about them."[3]

Women working together has long been celebrated in the oral and written history of this country by the quilting bee—an activity that is viewed as distinctively American in origin and scope. Its essentially indigenous nature was highlighted by several well-known writers in the nineteenth century, Frances Trollope (see second epigraph above) among them. Richard Weston, a bookseller from Edinburgh, also commented on this uniquely American event and describes in great detail a quilting bee (as well as an apple bee) that he attended in upstate New York in the 1830s:

The ladies began to assemble and take their seats before sundown, each having provided herself with quilting needles, thread being furnished to them; a pasteboard pattern was used to form the dicing, which was drawn on the cloth with chalk. After sundown, the gentlemen began to arrive, and took their seats at a respectful distance from the ladies; but as their fair dames knew there was no such ceremony in my country, I was allowed a greater latitude, and sat between two of them....[4]

And in 1849 Fredrika Bremer, a Swedish novelist visiting the United States, highlighted the oft-times humanitarian aspect of these communal gatherings in her explanation of a bee in a letter to a friend:

If a family is reduced to poverty by fire or sickness, and the children are in want of clothes or anything else, a number of ladies of the neighborhood...immediately get together...and sew for them. Such a sewing assembly is called a *bee*! And now there was a bee...to sew for a family who had lost all their clothing through fire, and I was invited to be present at it.[5]

The exchange of sewing and quilting labor was a regular part of the everyday work life of women during the Colonial period of this country, and these activities were sometimes enlivened by refreshments and light festivities, but the larger and more organized gatherings that we think of today as "quilting bees" do not appear to have become common until some time early in the nineteenth century. In fact, the term "bee" only began to be applied to quilting parties at about the turn of that century and, interestingly enough, was first applied by men—quite possibly as a carryover from such male-dominated activities as husking bees and logging bees. Women's diaries and letters consistently refer to their gatherings as "quiltings," "quilting frolics," or sometimes simply as "frolics" (occasionally spelled as "frolicks"), although they used the term "bee" for other communal events:

In February, 1805, we settled upon a farm near Batavia....Some of our earliest parties were got up by first designating the log house of some settler, and each one contributing to the entertainment; one would carry some flour, another some sugar, another some eggs, another some butter, and so on; the aggregate making a rustic feast. These parties would alternate from house to house. Frolics in the evening would uniformly attend *husking bees*, [barn or house] raisings, *quiltings*, and pumpkin parings.[6] [emphasis mine]

By the mid-nineteenth century, however, "bee" had become the commonly accepted terminology by women as well as men, although "quilting" is still used in some areas even today. (The terms are used interchangeably here.)

Although the concept of exchange work was well ingrained in society, the opportunity to work together was

16. *The Quilting Frolic*, John Krimmel, oil on canvas. The quilt is finished and is being removed from the frame as neighbors arrive for the evening festivities. (Courtesy Henry Francis du Pont Winterthur Museum, Winterthur, Delaware)

17. *The Quilting Party*; Elizabeth Williams Morgan; Buffalo, New York; c. 1861; hickory nuts, silk, wood, painted cast iron. (Buffalo and Erie County Historical Society, Buffalo, New York) A group of home-made dolls in silk period dresses and with hickory-nut heads are seated around a tiny quilt tied to a quilting frame. Most of the figures have needles in their hands, ready to quilt. The chairs are of painted cast iron and the miniature quilting frame rests on them much as a full-size one would at a quilting party of the time.

12

as important for its social aspects as for the work accomplished. Not only would quilting parties allow women to contribute their sewing skills to help out friends, relatives, and neighbors, but they also allowed time for exchange of news and opinions as their fingers busily carried out the day's work. Friendships then, as today, were forged over the quilting frame, engagements announced, leavetakings acknowledged, hospitality exchanged, and neighborly interest and good will—the basis for a community—reaffirmed.

In many parts of the country, bees might be almost the only real social diversion—and the most popular—that women had open to them. As one New England farm woman indicated, the sole saving features of an otherwise monotonous and colorless existence were the quilting bees she attended.[7] She mentioned helping at twenty-eight "quiltings" over one winter; in addition, she made a quilt herself and helped her neighbors on an informal basis with theirs. The hunger for social interaction that bees could satisfy (often for men as well as women) are evident in diary entries and letters; they were often the first social events held by women in remote frontier areas or as a welcome break in a long and difficult winter: "Today was a quilting at Montgomeris, the whole Neighborhood was invited, and a great many was there present, I kept house and let go nearly all the Gentlemen."[8] "February 7—We have had deep snow. No teams passed for over three weeks, but as soon as the drifts could be broken through Mary Scott sent her boy Frank around to say she was going to have a quilting. Everybody turned out...."[9] The ubiquitousness of bees as social diversions by the end of the century was such that Mary Wilkins Freeman would write:

One sometimes wonders whether it will ever be possible in our village to attain absolute rest and completion with regard to quilts. One thinks after a week fairly swarming with quilting bees, "now every housewife in the place must be well supplied; there will be no need to make more quilts for six months at least." Then, the next morning a nice little becurled girl in a clean white pinafore knocks at the door and demurely repeats her well-conned lesson: "Mother sends her compliments, and would be happy to have you come to her quilting bee this afternoon."[10]

Descriptions of quilting bees and their accompanying festivities abound.[11] Weston makes the point that the anticipation was as much a part of the bee as the actual activity:

The gentlemen...were as silent as if they had been figures of wax.... The scene was strange, but I knew that fun and kissing were coming, and that the real bee was in their minds, though at present lying dormant. The quilt was finished in about three hours, and taken down, hands washed, the frame put away,

and the room swept. A fiddler...was engaged, and he could play well; refreshments were handed round....[12]

He goes on to tell in great detail of the games and dances that followed the quilting bee. He also makes clear that quilting was a *women's* activity—the men were relegated to the background until after the quilt was taken from the frame. Other accounts, both factual and fictional, of these large bees, for which socialization seemed as much or more the motivation than the work, also comment extensively on the array of food and drink, often provided cooperatively, and the range of play:

My girls had some neighbors to help them quilt a bed quilt, 15 ladies...finisht and took it out at 7, evening. There were 12 gentlemen took tea. They danced a little after supper. Behaved exceedingly cleverly.[13]

Pies, cakes, preserves, and Hyson tea, with large lumps of loaf sugar, were provided liberally for the occasion.[14]

One basket was devoted to cakes of every species... pats of golden butter curiously stamped, reposing on a bed of fresh green leaves...currants, red and white, and delicious cherries and raspberries...cold fowl and tongue delicately prepared, and shaded with feathers of parsley...a long table stood exhibiting all the multitude of provision.... Unrestrained gayeties followed,...and all the gallantries of the times were enacted.[15]

Cookies and cider were handed about, when they gathered in the barn, And the lassies' dainty fingers flew, while the lads told many a yarn....[16]

A general description of the festivities that accompanied anything from barn raisings to quiltings was provided by an Ohio judge, who noted that there would be "a hearty dinner and a supper...[followed by] the inevitable dance,...which would be kept up to the music of the fiddle with little cessation, 'til near the break of day.'"[17]

Perhaps because women were seldom able to get together in large groups for the sheer pleasure of conversation, bees became trading grounds of information and news. They also gained a reputation through the years as perfect "nests of gossip" and slander, and several nineteenth-century stories (often written by men) are representative of this common perception:

The conversation...was not very aesthetic, literary, scientific, or instructive. The women...had but little time to read, or to think of much, except domestic and church affairs, together with the faults and foibles of their friends and neighbors....So, as the busy needles pierced the quilt, the busy tongues, sharp as needles, pierce the characters of the absent.[18]

18. "A Quilting Party in Western Virginia," *Gleason's Pictorial Drawing Room Companion*, October 1854, p. 249. (Courtesy America Hurrah Antiques, New York City)

19. *The Quilting Bee*; Grandma Moses; oil on canvas; 1950; 20″ x 24″. Copyright © 1989, Grandma Moses Properties Co., New York. This charming memory painting captures the essence of the pervasive mythology of a quilting bee on a grand scale—some women diligently working at the quilting frame and others busily preparing the repast soon to be placed on the waiting table, while men, children, and other women talk, play, or carry out other tasks as they, too, await the festivities that will follow the quilting.

20. One member of a quilting party diligently works while others take a gossip break. (Collections of Library of Congress, Washington, D.C.)

14

I always make a pint of going to quiltings, for you can't be backbited to your face, that's a moral serenty....Quiltin' just set wimmen to slanderin' as easy and beautiful as anything you ever see'.[19]

On the positive side, Gibbons notes that "we quilted and rolled, laughed and talked....At this quilting I heard but little gossip, and less scandal."[20] Gossip was indeed exchanged at bees, and probably biting criticism also played its part, but the sociability of the event also allowed women to deal with the very real problems and concerns of their daily lives in an acceptable manner, and issues of child care, housekeeping, marital relations, community service, births, weddings, deaths, politics, and crises of every order could be brought into the open, reviewed, discussed, and decisions made with the support of a peer group. In a very real sense, bees may have served as the first women's consciousness-raising sessions.

While much of the rhetoric relating to quilting bees and parties probably most closely concerned middle-class or better-off women, such friendly gatherings were not exclusive to any one segment of the population. Those in the poorest rural areas might not have the elaborate entertainments and refreshments described in many stories and poems, but although the entertainment may have derived mostly from the gossip passed, and the food and drink been part of the regular family fare, the cooperative and supportive spirit shown was no less important. As Sarah Connell Ayer noted in her diary for August 14, 1809,

"in the afternoon I went to Mrs. Ayer's...to assist in quilting...we had a cheerful, pleasant time. I enjoyed it far better than any visit of ceremony."[21]

Slaves were also participants in this truly American activity. Sewing was a heavy responsibility on southern plantations, for the mistress of the plantation had to clothe and provide bedding not only for her own family but for the plantation slaves as well.[22] A slave who could sew well was highly valued and often worked closely with the mistress in creating items of fine needlework as well as producing everyday items. Many of the exquisitely appliquéd and quilted plantation quilts that we admire today carry the work of the silent fingers of those women, who may have worked side by side with their mistresses in creating these objects of beauty that they would never use.[23]

Most slave women also supplemented their families' meager clothing and bedding allotments with hours of sewing after their regular work was done. Making quilts with scraps and fabrics gleaned from their mistresses and worn-out clothes or purchased with what few funds they might have was an important part of this after-hours stitchery, and all members of the family would be pressed into service to help. Former slaves that were interviewed as part of the WPA Federal Writers' Project in the 1930s also told of informal, slave-organized bees where this work was carried out:

One of the most enjoyable affairs in those days was the quilting party. Every night they would assemble

"THE 'BROTHERS' ASSISTED IN THE QUILTING."

21. "The Brothers Assisted in the Quilting"; wood engraving from *Harper's Weekly*, April 21, 1883. Photograph courtesy Historic New Orleans Collection, Acc. No. 1979.122, New Orleans, Louisiana.

at some particular house and help that person finish her quilts. The next night, a visit would be made to someone else's home, and so on, until everyone had a sufficient amount of bed-clothing for winter. Besides, this was an excellent chance to get together for a pleasant time and discuss the latest gossip.[24]

These gatherings provided some relief from the endless oppressive work and insecurity that the slaves faced every day. They helped to create a sense of community in an often unstable environment and gave women the opportunity to create bonds of mutual support, bonds that quite possibly helped to sustain them in a life that often saw parents, child, sibling, or spouse sold away from them, perhaps never to be seen again.

As in white groups, the women were always in control of the quiltings, whether they were spontaneous gatherings or organized events. Children were, by necessity, allowed but expected to stay quiet and out of the way unless asked to help with something. Men were invited; they might thread needles, hold candles, be around for dancing and games, escort women home, or keep the fire alive, but they were there on the women's sufferance. However, as one respondent to the WPA surveys said, "Mens had a good time at quiltin's too."[25]

The slaves usually arranged their own refreshments for these gatherings ("Dem colla'd greens wid cornpone an' plenty of ginger cakes an' fruit puffs an' big old pots of coffee wuz mighty fine eatin' to us den"[26]). The dancing and games that sometimes followed these quiltings (or "sprees," as they were also called) paralleled what happened at white quiltings. Fry describes a ring play that is quite similar to one described by Weston in his lively description of the activities following a quilting in the 1830s,[27] but other games and music grew from African traditions.

Today the quilting tradition remains strong among black women for both work and pleasure. Some women have turned working together much to their advantage; the Freedom Quilting Bee (now called the Martin Luther King, Jr., Freedom Quilting Bee), established in 1966, has given poor black women in one Alabama county an opportunity to use their very substantial skills to supplement otherwise meager incomes.[28] This group, many of whom had initially quilted together through church connections (One says, "I was always with the choir members 'cause the choir members would be together quilting. We had a lot of fun around the quilts, sometimes cooking and eating, too."[29]), formed a cooperative they called the Freedom Quilting Bee. The group went through some lean periods in the course of establishing itself (As one woman recalls, "Sometimes we wasn't getting nothing out of the quilts. Working to get it some day."[30]), but

eventually their work meant not only a better standard of living but also an increase in self-esteem and belief in each other.

By the late nineteenth century, quilting bees had changed in nature and character; working together to help each other was less of a necessity and more opportunities for social interchange were available, eliminating the usefulness of bees as a place for young men and women to meet and have lively social interchange. Bees became almost entirely single-sex affairs, the work often devoted to the making of fundraisers or presentation pieces. Although refreshments might still be served, the advent of men to partake of food, fun, and games when the work was done became almost a relic of the past. "Bee" also began to be applied more generally; it was used to refer to almost any gathering of women where quilting was done, whatever the reason and whether or not food and entertainment formed a part of the activity. Even contemporary magazines bemoaned the lost charm of the bees of earlier years and, for the benefit of readers who may never have attended one, carefully spelled out in their stories what these earlier gatherings had been like.

Group quiltings today are also less "bees" in the traditional sense; they are usually more purposeful and organized, and motivations for participation often range far beyond the need for exchange work and those early yearnings for companionship and sharing. In many areas they are still closely tied to church or grange activities and remain essentially a female-only activity. In only a few, however, is the idea of exchange work at all part of the reason for attending; companionship, however, remains an underlying factor. The quilts produced are still most often fundraisers or presentation gifts, or they are made to bring attention to social or political concerns. In several groups, quilting may also be done for hire, usually to raise money for church functions or other needs. Quilt guilds, which have rapidly proliferated in recent years, now also often fill the niche that bees once did; through their meetings, they provide both the opportunity for those who so desire to work together and a forum for the exchange of ideas or just plain small talk.

Even though the heyday of the traditional quilting bee is long in the past, and today's manifestations may take a different form, women have continued through the years to gather together to make quilts, conversation, and joy, and there is every indication that they will continue to do so in the future. Whether they now work together for the fun of it or to accomplish specific tasks, the supportive memory of those lively gatherings of yesteryear still surrounds today's activities with a serendipitous glow, and participants lend their hands secure in the knowledge that they are playing their part in the continuing evolution of a unique American phenomenon.

22. *The Quilting Bee*; M. C. 5¢ Jones; water-color, pencil, and ballpoint pen on paper; 1991; 10″ x 12″. Photograph by Gavin Ashworth. (Collection of Cathy Rasmussen)

23. *Finishing the Quilt*; Nan Phelps; Hamilton, Ohio; oil on canvas; 1980; 28½″ x 44¼″. (Collection of Museum of American Folk Art, New York City; Donated by Robert Phelps in loving memory of his wife, Nan Phelps. 1992.18.1)

24. Album top (Primitive Hall Quilt top); members of the Pennock family; Marlborough Township, Chester County, Pennsylvania; 1842–1843; pieced cotton with ink drawings and inscriptions; 66″ x 66″. Photograph courtesy Henry Francis du Pont Winterthur Museum, Winterthur, Delaware. (Collection of Chester County Historical Society, West Chester, Pennsylvania) A genealogical block (top row, center) provides a wealth of family history as well as the information that the top was given to two-year-old Sarah Wister Pennock, daughter of Caroline Morris Pennock and Caspar Wistar Pennock, two of the makers. Inscribed on the pages of the book in this block are the names of recent generations of the Pennock and Morris families, and on the spine is the legend "C.W. Pennock/ to his/ Daughter/ 1842." The centerpiece of the top is a drawing of Primitive Hall, the ancestral home of the Pennocks. The elaborate and precise geometric blocks are all the more intriguing because of the lack of published patterns at the time, but the Pennocks, who were Quakers, had undoubtedly been well-educated and were skilled in the use of ruler, compass, and straight edge, as well as in calligraphy and drawing.

18

A Family Affair

"In the country life of America there are many moments when a woman can have recourse to nothing but her needle for employment."[1]

"Wednesday Aunt Marsh came up and would have me go quilt for Cousin Anna Hubbard I went...."[2]

"I can remember in the wintertime, we all would be working on quilts. I... was the youngest and my mother would have me making running stitches near the edges because my arms were too short....We had a way of working as follows:

Robert Berry—Stepfather—longest arms.
Mary Berry—Mother—next longest arms.
Otho Hamer—Brother—next longest arms.
Lenora Hamer—sister—next longest arms.
Ernestine Hamer—shortest arms."[3]

In spite of the nostalgia generated by oral tradition, paintings, stories, poems, and song, there is much to indicate that the large and lively gatherings depicted were the exception rather than the rule, especially in the earliest years of this nation. Shared quilting then probably most often occurred on a much smaller scale, as strictly a family affair or with the help of close friends and neighbors (who often were peripherally related and treated as part of a larger extended family, whether or not a true blood relationship existed), who simply acted as good neighbors would—helping out when and where help was needed. And, if part of the helping allowed for a respite from their own heavy loads of work—leisure was almost an unknown concept in the Colonial and frontier environments, even among the wealthier classes—and for a little light social interaction, so much the better!

Families were closeknit in those early days and relied heavily on members to carry out all the work that needed to be done. Everyone was expected to do their fair share at home as well as to help others as needed, as Elizabeth Porter Phelps noted above. Work was most often reciprocal, but occasionally even family members might be paid to complete some especially onerous needlework task. Diaries from these early years frequently refer to relatives and neighbors informally visiting each other and helping with sewing and quilting, and Phelps, for example, has numerous references in her diaries, spanning more than forty years (1763-1812), to her relatives, as well as neighbors, helping each other quilt: "Tuesday morning I went to quilt on a quilt for my Aunt Porter—we finished the quilt before 11....Wednesday I at Brother's to help Sister Quilt..."; "Thursday sister Warner and Mrs. Ship-

man here to help me Quilt a Bed quilt for Porter, Fryday here again."[4]

Such information as has come down to us through the years indicates that quilting was incorporated on a regular basis into the everyday work routine of family life. In homes large enough to allow it, a quilting frame containing a work in progress was almost always in place, encouraging the women in the family to sit down and stitch whenever the opportunity arose. (It also meant that any visiting ladies could find gainful occupation while discoursing with the women of the house.) In less well-off areas and homes, women within the immediate family would do piecework, sometimes alone, sometimes together, until one or several tops were ready to quilt; then the frame would be set up and other relatives or neighbors would join the family in finishing work on the quilts.[5] In either case, quilting as a household activity was differentiated from quilting as a social event. Refreshments and a little light play might occasionally attend the family quilting; Frances Baylor Hill of Virginia, for example, describes several days in 1797 when an aunt's quilt was on the frame and she, along with other relatives and neighbors, stopped by as they could to help quilt, thus making a constantly changing number of helping hands. On one day, she noted, they "quilt'd a great deal and was very merry," and on another day they "spent the day agreeable eating drinking and quilting."[6] But what marked a quilting as a truly social event was, first, the invited presence of men, and second, the intentional inclusion of a larger group than immediate family.

The companionship that could accompany this work (and hard work it was, no matter what social discourse

25. If there wasn't room in the house to set up the quilting frame, women simply moved outside. (Collections of Library of Congress, Washington, D.C.)

26. Presidential Wreath, members of the Traver family; Sand Lake, New York; mid-nineteenth century; pieced and appliquéd cotton; 96″ x 96″. (Collection of Shelburne Museum, Shelburne, Vermont; Gift of Kitty Webb Harris) "Washington's Reception by the Ladies..., on passing the bridges at Trenton, NJ...," an 1845 Currier & Ives lithograph that commemorates Washington's inaugural parade in 1789, shows women with rose wreaths in their hair throwing flowers in front of the procession as it makes its way through rose-bedecked streets and is thought to have been the inspiration for the Presidential Wreath pattern. The pattern, a favorite of the mid-nineteenth century both for individual blocks in album quilts and for repetitious presentations as shown here, is thought to have originated in New Jersey. The appliqué work in this beautifully executed example of the pattern was probably done by one woman, with other family members assisting in the joining and quilting of the blocks.

20

27. Counterpane; possibly made by Mary Willing Byrd and Elizabeth Bassett Harrison; Westover and Berkeley Plantations, James City County, Virginia; 1780–1800; appliquéd and embroidered cotton, linen; 105½″ x 97¾″. (Collection of Valentine Museum, Richmond, Virginia; Gift of Tazewell Ellett) Although not a quilt in the true sense of the word (there is no batting and quilting), this piece is an excellent example of the needlework popular at the time. According to the donor, this counterpane was made by the wives of the owners of adjacent plantations, and family lore has it not only that these two women met frequently to sew, but also that these neighboring families had an almost continuous informal bee going in which family members would frequently be at each other's homes to work together.

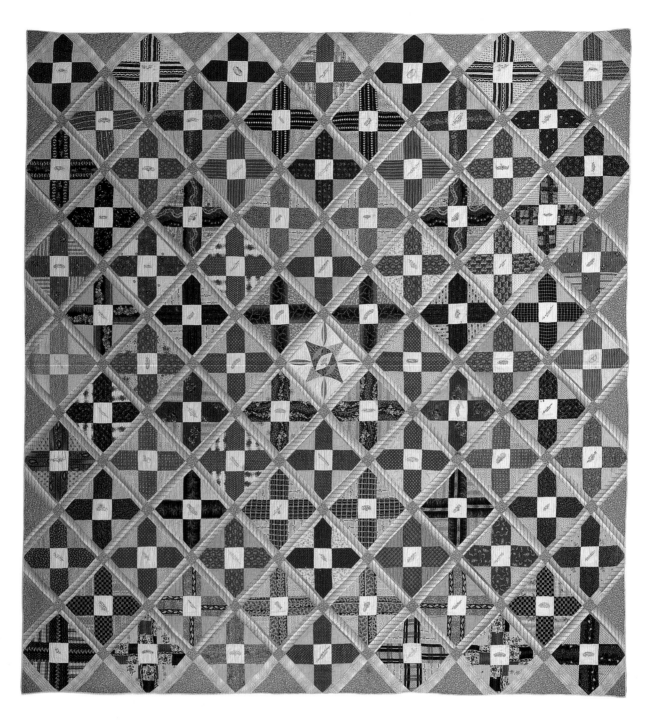

28. Snow Flake Signature; members of the Phillips family; Phillips Mill, Bucks County, Pennsylvania; c. 1845; 106″ x 103″. (Collection of The Mercer Museum of The Bucks County Historical Society, Doylestown, Pennsylvania) Snow Flake, along with Chimney Sweep, was a popular pattern for friendship quilts in the mid-1800s. This one contains eighty-five signatures, some handwritten and others stamped with decorative metal dies. Many of the blocks were signed by members of the Phillips family, which had built a mill in 1756 in the hamlet that took their name and then operated it for four generations. Although its history is not known, the quilt was most likely made for a family member, perhaps on the occasion of a marriage.

might surround it) probably did much to promote the frequent interaction among family members living in reasonable proximity. Neighboring families (whether or not related), especially in the South, apparently took full advantage of the possibilities for interchange that quilting offered: "Women of the Stewart and Burgess families were, in fact, members of a floating quilting bee that seemed ever to be in session at one or another of the families' farms.... They were made for the most utilitarian of reasons, and they were made for special occasions. Above all else, they were made as a joint effort of the Stewart and Burgess women."[7] The Harrison and Byrd families, living on the Berkeley and Westover plantations in Virginia, were known to have had a similar interchange; the exquisite Broderie Perse quilt illustrated in figure 27 was made by this family group and is representative of a style favored in the southern colonies in the late eighteenth and early nineteenth centuries.

The extreme interdependence that the settlement patterns and shared work habits of the seventeenth to nineteenth centuries generated often made it exceptionally hard for family members to separate, and women seemed to find separation the most difficult. Often the best friends a woman had were other women within her family; she relied on them for moral and emotional support, for help in times of crisis, for extra helping hands when work needed to be done.[8] In fact, when such

expected help was not forthcoming, a peevish note might even enter into the voices of these women:

I have put a bed quilt into the frame and you know that must be a tedious job. The quilt was commenced by Mr. Ambler's mother and I think I am bound to finish it. Catherine and Elizabeth Ambler are staying with me and they occasionally assist me though not much....[9]

1851 Friday... made an effort to get on with my much talked of quilt, but with no assistance, it was very laborious, and I was almost sorry I undertook it.[10]

These ties were perhaps even more important when other female friendship was less readily available—or even nonexistent, as in some remote parts of the frontier—and often a woman would invite a sister, aunt, or cousin to live with her even after marriage, as much for companionship as for the additional help. Again, diaries have given great insight into the significance of these bonds among the female members of a family and some sense of the loss felt when a woman found it necessary—usually because of marriage—to leave the supportive circle of close and dear relatives. This was especially evident during the westward expansion and migration of the nineteenth century, as women, uprooted from the extended families and familiar locations in which they

29. Album; members of the Snook family; Fishkill, New York; c. 1860; pieced and appliquéd cotton; 91″ x 77″. Photograph by Scott Bowron courtesy New York Quilt Project, Museum of American Folk Art, New York City. (Collection of Fishkill Historical Society, Fishkill, New York) Eleven of the thirty blocks in this quilt are signed, and many of the signers appear to be related, as they read "Cousin Julia," "Cousin Emily," and so forth. The quilt descended in the Snook family and is considered a family album; genealogical research corroborates this belief.

30. Crazy; members of the More family; Oakland area, California; pieced and embroidered cotton velvet; 54″ x 66″. (Courtesy The Oakland Museum History Department, Acc. # H70.32.1, Oakland, California) The More children, under the supervision of their mother, probably had a lot of fun as they made this delightful quilt as a Christmas present for their grandmother. The quilt contains an amazing collection of farm and wild animals and birds, favored pets, and various mementoes. The three boys embroidered on the quilt may represent the More children, but no explanation is known for the many clocks depicted.

had been reared, faced an uncertain future as they prepared to settle in new and unfamiliar areas without benefit of the supports to which they were accustomed:

April 1838. If I were to yield to inclination I should cry half the time without knowing why. So much danger attends me…a long journey yet before me, going I know not whither; without mother or sister to attend me can I survive it all?[11]

Nothing can atone for the loss of the society of friends.…I cannot make a friend like mother out of Henry.[12]

The companionable familial closeness lost in such moves was one of the first elements that women would attempt to reestablish once their new situations would allow. Sewing and quilting, so intimate a part of family life and interaction, were often means that women used to bring them together with others in order to retrieve a sense of that combination of fellowship and work, and sororal companionship in this area was replaced with the development of relations with unrelated women in greater proximity to each other as the country reached its full expanse of settlement.

By the mid- to late-nineteenth century, sewing and missionary societies—some church related, others community sponsored—and a host of other groups devoted to benevolent and social activism began to play their part in providing women with surrogate relationships for the close family bonds that were, in many cases, no longer available to them. In this century, the family model tended even more toward the nuclear rather than the extended group, and guilds and other often more socially oriented groups also offered women some of the closer ties—both in companionship and shared work—that were lacking when family members were scattered far and wide.

The Great Depression of the 1930s brought families together in new ways as many were forced to reconsolidate during a tough economic period; these years saw a brief resurgence in family members working together again on quilts—quilting in general went through a brief revival period then—and the reasons ranged from the purely economic to the need to keep occupied. With the end of the Great Depression, most families were more than happy to return to the patterns of commercial consumption established earlier and to reinstate family ties through other activities.

Today, family quilting in most parts of the country has almost disappeared. Sewing and quilting are no longer the necessary household chores they once were, and proximity of relatives has dramatically changed over the years. In a few isolated areas, extended family networks are still very much in evidence and familial reciprocity, whether in quilting or other work, still has its place. Irwin, for example, in writing about southern Appalachia, notes that even in recent years several women in the same family would often get together to quilt, and Cooper and Buferd, in interviews with southwestern women, quote one, as follows: "Everyone put their hand to piecing in the winter. All my boys pieced right along with the girls. It was work that had to be done."[13] However, the preponderance of families now have members scattered across the country; reunions might bring them together and work on a collaborative project might occur, but the daily familial work interaction of earlier times is, for the most part, a nostalgic memory.

31. Amish Irish Chain variation; makers unknown; Holmes County, Ohio; c. 1910; pieced cotton face, wool backing; 80″ x 68″. Photograph by Scott Bowron. (Courtesy Susan Parrish Antiques, New York City) The family working together is an informal but strong tradition in Amish culture, and it is thought that this quilt was the result of such a joint effort, perhaps made for a member going to another community or even for an "english" (or non-Amish) friend. The design is a familiar one, but the unusual touch is the series of initials that are embroidered within the middle three rows of large diamonds, top to bottom—something rarely seen in Amish quilts as it was a touch that was considered too "worldly." A story is told of a Friendship quilt made by an Amish group that actually had sayings such as "Remember Me" embroidered on it, but the minister in whose church it was made caused several of the sayings to be ripped out for being too worldly (see *Sunshine and Shadow* by Phyllis Haders).

32. Oak Leaf Cluster; made by family and friends of Mary Jane Dykes; Philadelphia, Pennsylvania, environs; 1845–1847; pieced and appliquéd cotton; 117″ x 108″. (Photograph by Karen Bell courtesy Laura Fisher/Antique Quilts and Americana, New York City) Made as a wedding gift, this quilt carries the names of both the bride, Mary Jane Dykes, and the groom, Thomas Watson, who were married in Philadelphia on December 16, 1847. Mary Jane came from a family of German Quakers, and the quilt is a good example of those made by Quaker communities as gifts for their members. Each block carries a different signature, and on some the signatures appear within decorative stamps. The bride's mother, Cynthia Dykes, included an inscription with her block: "Let all things be done/ decently and in order./ Corinth. 14 Chap. 40 vs."

Matrimony Must Even Be Tried

"Not having had trouble
enough, *Matrimony*
must even be tried."

"To marry, or not to marry,
that's the question."

"There is one good wife
in the country, &
every man thinks
he hath her."
—From Clara Willson Coleman's
Album Quilt, 1862

"*March 26, 1862:* I have been up at Laura Chapin's from 10 o'clock in the morning until 10 at night, finishing Jennie Howell's bed quilt, as she is to be married very soon. Almost all of the girls were there. We finished it at 8 p.m. and when we took it off the frames we gave three cheers. Some of the youth of the village came up to inspect our handiwork and see us home.

"*July 15, 1866:* It kept the girls busy to get Abby Clark's quilt and mine finished within one month. They hope the rest of the girls will postpone their nuptials till there is a change in the weather. Mercury stands 90 degrees in the shade."[1]

Prior to the twentieth century, marriage marked a role shift of major significance in a woman's life. The transition from girl to adult, from maiden to wife and mother was a move both expected and sought, desired and sometimes feared; it could mean more independence or less, an exchange of one set of housekeeping duties for another or an opportunity to broaden horizons. In the closeknit and static life of preindustrial America, it almost inevitably meant a period of upheaval as a girl sought to adapt to her new status in life. If there were supportive women nearby in this transition period—be they relatives or friends—it could make the adjustment much easier, but for those women who found themselves uprooted, moving to new communities or heading for an uncertain life on the western frontier without the support of their peers, the change could be wrenching and difficult. Perhaps the real reason that so many women chose to wed within their own familiar community was not only the close availability of the men, but also the possibility of carrying over into their married life the familial and friendly ties that had been established in their earlier life. The ability to retain the comfort of these customary relationships would no doubt make the transition to the new state less abrupt and help to maintain a continuity that was highly valued.[2]

Whether a woman left the community or stayed, a gift of a quilt from those closest to her could both commemorate this significant event in her life and serve as a reminder of her place among the group that cared for and supported her. Examples range from highly elaborate Album quilts to simple repetitive block quilts; yet, regardless of the wealth of design or the simplicity of execution, care and affection as well as the desire to give a lasting and useful gift are evident. Nicoll notes that Quakers were especially fond of weddings as events to commemorate with quilts.[3] This is in line with the strong emphasis that Quakers placed on the importance of community both in the basic tenets of their faith and in their everyday life. To the Quakers, making a quilt together was not only a confirmation of community but also a tangible reminder to the recipients that they were but one part of the many social relationships that make up the whole.

Although men might participate to a certain extent in the making of a marriage quilt—although rarely involved in the actual making, they often added their penmanship or other calligraphic skills to the finished product—and although some quilts are known to have been made specifically for the groom, the wedding quilt remained by and large a gift by and from women to women. The quilt was not simply a reification of the community at large but very much an acknowledgment of the bonds of women as well.

Folklore is rich in traditions allied to courtship, engagements, marriage, and quilting, some passed down orally in families and others captured in the popular literature of the nineteenth and early twentieth centuries.[4] Surprisingly, most early diaries do not bear out the existence of such traditions; Richards' diary aside, Bonfield's research, for example, has shown a lack of specific references to betrothal or wedding quilts, as well as the customs assumed to be associated with their making. Her research has, however, uncovered numerous entries that allude to an increase in quilting activity near wedding times, implying that at least some of the quilting going on was related to the upcoming nuptials, whether particularly stated or not.[5]

One of the long-held popular beliefs reflected in several nineteenth-century works of fiction is that a quilting was often given to announce a betrothal.[6] Another has it that many young girls pieced and appliquéd quilt tops for their hope chests, then put them away until they became engaged, at which time their neighbors would be invited to help with the finishing of them. These tops might range from the simple to the elaborate, and, so the tradition goes, often the best top was quilted only by friends, the bride-to-be not being allowed to take part in its finishing for fear of bad luck. According to Hinson, this latter tradition was an outgrowth of a custom dating back to the 1700s, when a girl would ask friends to help make her wedding quilt, and this then grew into a belief that it would be bad luck for the bride-to-be to work on it herself.[7] Yet other stories tell of "jumping the cat"—when a quilt was taken from the frame, the unmarried girls who had worked on it would hold it up while a cat was tossed into the center of the quilt. Whichever girl was closest to the cat when it jumped out of the quilt would be the next to marry—or so the stories go!

Also part of the quilting mythology is the notion of a "baker's dozen" of quilts that were made as part of a girl's dowry, with the thirteenth quilt being the "special" or most elaborate one. A short story by T. S. Arthur published in *Godey's Lady's Book* in 1849 indicates that a smaller number of quilts might also be acceptable, if no less necessary: "[in our younger days] half a dozen handsome patchwork quilts were indispensable then as a marriage portion…,"[8] and an amusing tale by George Washington Harris tells of a woman who had over twenty quilts that she had made and "she ment tu give evry durn'd one ove them to Sal [her daughter] when she got married."[9] A bee might be held for the express purpose of completing some or all of these quilt tops (often the most costly part of a quilt was the batt and backing, and a family would not invest in this part until the quilts were actually going to be needed) or for only the "special" quilt. Harriet Beecher Stowe, in her 1859 story "The

33. Kentucky Rose Variation; Elizabeth Daniel Poindexter, Martha Poindexter, Verlinda Poindexter, Susan Poindexter, Elizabeth "Bettie" Poindexter, and Sally E. Poindexter; Boonville area, Cooper County, Missouri; 1852; appliquéd cotton with embroidery and stuffed work; 104″ x 83⅜″. (Collection of DAR Museum, Washington, D.C.; Gift of Mrs. T.L. Tolbert) This pretty quilt, with its delicate roses and quilted and stuffed doves, served twice as a wedding gift. It was originally made for Mary Ann Poindexter by her mother and three sisters for Mary Ann's marriage to Dr. John Marshall Staples on September 30, 1852, and the quilt carries a lightly stuffed quilted inscription reading "Mary Ann Poindexter 1852/ John Marshall Staples." Family lore notes that Mary Ann was not allowed to work on the quilt, which her relatives made during her "courting" days, because that would have brought bad luck. Dr. Staples died during the Civil War, and Mary Ann later presented the quilt to her sister Bettie (who was only nine years old when she worked on the quilt for her older sister) on the occasion of her marriage to William Parks Gunn in 1872.

34. Double Tie; members of the Young Ladies Sewing Society; Canandaigua, New York; 1865; pieced cotton; 76″ x 74½″. (Collection of Ontario County Historical Society, Canandaigua, New York) This quilt, made for Mary Field, who married P. Willis Fisk (or Fiske), is possibly one of the first made by the group of young women, immortalized in Caroline Cowles Richards' diary, who agreed to make a quilt for each member of the group as she got married. An old label attached to the back of the quilt noted that "Many of [Mary Field's] girl friends who had attended the Old Canandaigua Female Academy with her thought it would be fun to piece a block for a quilt, with their names and a verse in the center of the block, then sew all the blocks together and quilt them onto a backing and present it to her on her wedding day as a surprise. This was done, and it was indeed a great surprise to Mary Field, who always thereafter called it her 'Friendship Quilt.'" Given that Richards was quite explicit about the agreement that the girls in the group had made, the surprise may not have been as great as reported by family tradition!

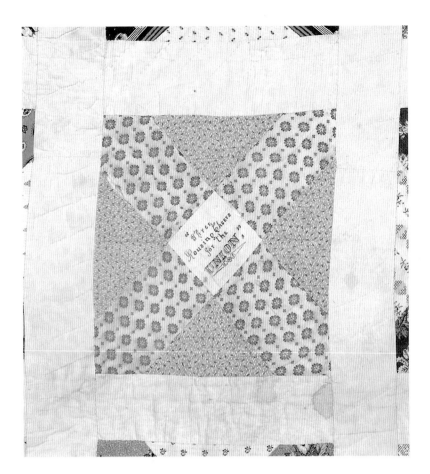

34a. Detail of Double Tie quilt.

Minister's Wooing," captures both the concept of a quilting to announce an engagement and the choosing of a "special" top for the quilting:

> The quilting was in those days considered as the most solemn and important recognition of a betrothal.... When a wedding was forthcoming, then there was a solemn review of the stores of beauty and utility thus provided, and the patchwork-spread best worthy of such distinction was chosen for the quilting.... Thereto, duly summoned, trooped all intimate female friends of the bride, and the quilt being spread on a frame, and wadded with cotton, each vied with the other in the delicacy of the quilting they could put upon it; for quilting was also a fine art, and had its delicacies and nice points, concerning which grave, elderly matrons discussed with judicious care.[10]

Interviews in this century with women in rural areas of the South sometimes refute the idea that quilts were especially made for such occasions: "I don't remember any courtship quilts. The young girls weren't even interested. They didn't quilt anything fancy, just what was necessary. That was all they had time for."[11] However, it would seem obvious that only families that were somewhat better off financially could actually afford the luxury of working on and setting aside materials not immediately needed for use; in the poorer families—and many of the inhabitants of the rural South well into this century were extremely poor—the essentials of everyday life were often difficult enough to come by, and short-term day-to-day survival was of first consideration. It is also possible that some customs, even though part of a broad-based popular mythology, never existed in some areas or had simply died out and had not been retained as part of the oral tradition.

Regardless of whether the customs related to wedding quilts originated in fact or fiction, the reality is that many quilts known today were clearly made to celebrate the joining of community members, and their existence has enriched and enlivened the quilting heritage. The family lore that has come down with many quilts indicates that weddings were indeed considered a fine excuse for a quilting, and many quilts are said to have been created by friends and relatives to provide a warm token of love symbolic of the bonds of community.

One closeknit group of young women from Canandaigua, New York, many of whom had grown up together, played together, gone to school and church together, and supported each other through the rigors of the Civil War, had a pact to make such quilts for the members of their group. In the 1859 diary of Caroline Cowles Richards, one of the girls in the group, she noted that: "The young ladies have started a society....We are to meet once in two weeks and are to present each member with an album bed quilt with all our names on when they are married."[12] The

Young Ladies Sewing Society (also known as The Young Ladies Aid Society) was also meant to "cultivate, enrich, and enoblè [sic] our intellectual and moral natures, and to form habits of systematic benevolence..."; the records also note that "...forget not" was one of the goals contemplated by the group, a concept that fit very well into the ideal of friendship and women's ties in nineteenth-century America.[13]

Richards' diary, which covers a twenty-year period,

35. Double Tie; members of the Young Ladies Sewing Society; Canandaigua, New York; 1862; pieced cotton; 84″ x 72″. (Collection of Ontario County Historical Society, Canandaigua, New York) This quilt, also known as "Clara Wilson's Album Quilt," is another of those made by the Canandaigua group. This example, like the other quilts made for the group, carries a number of verses (some from Shakespeare) and quotations (many biblical) in addition to the signatures. One block makes a play on Clara's name: "Ah Clara! Clara! Listen! tarry!/ You Will-soon a Cole-man marry." Several of the blocks are also dated; one notes "The Happy Day/ Sept. 15, 1862," which was most probably Clara's wedding day. A label on the back carries the name "Clara E. Willson." Clara's name appears on Abbie Clark Richards' Flag quilt (see fig. 107) as "Clara Wilson [sic] Coleman."

36. Old Maid's Quilt; members of the Young Ladies Sewing Society; Canandaigua, New York; 1871; pieced and appliquéd cotton; 76″ x 68″. Photograph courtesy Shelly Zegart. (Collection of Los Angeles County Museum, Los Angeles, California) This quilt, made for Susan ("Susie") Elizabeth Daggett, personifies nineteenth-century attitudes toward women and marriage. The young women of the sewing society, many of whom had been at school with Susie at the Ontario Female Academy in Canandaigua, had agreed to make a quilt for each member of the society as she married, but when Susie announced her intention to stay single, the group nevertheless honored her with a quilt. It documents the esteem and affection in which she was held, while reflecting conflicting feelings about marriage and the single state: "T'is a very solemn thing to be married, but a great deal solemner [sic] not to be." The portrait is a stereotype; whether intentional or an "in" joke of the time, it can be construed to be an accurate picture of contemporary attitudes toward single women. (The minister of the church—not one of the girls—drew the picture.) Susie Daggett fulfilled her vow never to marry; she was active in church affairs, served as Assistant Lady Principal at Vassar College, and generally was fully engaged in living the life of her choice until she died in 1931 at the age of 89—time enough for her to have seen increasing options for women, including the right to vote.

makes frequent reference to the girls, their fiancés, and their wedding plans (as well as many aspects of everyday life), but she also takes note of one of the Society's members who had a different point of view: "Susie Daggett says she is never going to be married, but we must make her a quilt just the same."[14] Susie Daggett may have been the most vocal but perhaps not the only girl to override the prevalent mores and traditions of her time regarding marriage. It is of interest that, in spite of the prevalence of the belief in the "cult of true womanhood" that counted husband, home, and family as that to which all women should aspire, eleven of the forty-three girls whose names appear on the quilts made by this group ultimately remained spinsters.[15] Whether the significantly high number of unwed young women among this group was by choice (like Susie Daggett) or by chance is unknown. The Civil War undeniably severely depleted the ranks of eligible young men in the area (Richards' diary contains many references to local boys cut down in their prime), but other social forces of the times may also have been at work. Although the idea of women having options was still in the embryonic stage, relative economic affluence, the availability of education (many of these girls attended the Ontario Female Seminary in Canandaigua), and a growing receptivity to new and progressive social attitudes in the area made it possible for these young women to grow up with a greater awareness of the world than did their mothers. The area was also fairly close to Seneca Falls, the scene of the first feminist convention in 1848; when Susan B. Anthony came to speak to the women of Canandaigua in 1855, many of the younger girls also attended, and Richards' diary makes clear that Anthony's ideas made a strong impression on them.[16] Additionally, a concept known as the "Cult of Single Blessedness," rooted in Protestantism, had begun to make itself felt from around 1810 to 1860; it incorporated many of the elements seen as part of a woman's special sphere but offered a church-sanctioned alternative to marriage.[17]

The Sewing Society presented Susie Daggett with her quilt when she was thirty years old, and it is a time capsule of prevailing attitudes about the wed and unwed states. It is also the only quilt known to have been made for a member of the Society who remained unmarried; although later records indicated that any member of the Society who reached the age of thirty and was still unmarried was to receive a quilt, it is speculated that the biting sentiments expressed on the Daggett quilt, as well as the drawing on the central block was in all probability "the chief cause of this custom being forever abolished."[18] Several of the other quilts made for the girls in this group still exist; with the exception of the Daggett quilt, those known are of only two designs—a repetitive Double Tie pattern (two examples of which are illustrated in figures 34 and 35) that is ideal for signatures and sayings, and a Flag pattern (see fig. 107), made for those girls whose fiancés fought in the Civil War. Both styles are enlivened by delightful verses, patriotic sayings, and comments about marriage that the girls inked on them, but there is no doubt that the most acerbic commentary appears on the Daggett quilt.

In some ways, Freedom quilts for men may have served as wedding quilts in addition to their purpose of acknowledging a boy's coming of age. Dunton notes that Freedom quilts, like other testimonial quilts, were usually not meant for everyday use but were most often put away until the young man married.[19] Finley also says that a boy's Freedom quilt "always was laid carefully away against the time when he might add it as his gift to the dowry chest of his bride-to-be."[20] The parties that often accompanied the giving of these quilts may have been a means of announcing to the neighborhood that the boy being honored was now "marriageable," while allowing him the opportunity to establish a new level of interaction with young women whom his family would consider acceptable as mates. There are examples of other quilts made by young women specifically for unmarried men, but most of these were not Freedom quilts, as the men were frequently substantially older than twenty-one. They may have served a somewhat similar purpose, however, reminding the men of their duty to wed and offering a variety of potential candidates. One quilt of this type, documented by the Texas quilt project, was presented to twenty-six-year-old Thomas Chatman Simmons in 1885.[21] Family history has it that the quilt was made by local women, some of whom hoped to marry the eligible young man, a recent newcomer to the area. He undoubtedly disappointed them, however, as he returned to his home state of Georgia to find a wife.

Although the group-made quilt as a wedding gift has declined in popularity in recent years, it is still a tradition that has far from disappeared and today is appearing in new forms. In a recent version, when Susan Shie, a well-known contemporary quilter, married in 1991, quilting friends from around the world sent her individual blocks that ranged from the romantic to the humorous. Many of the blocks were pinned together for a wedding-day display, and they now adorn her house in decorative groupings. Thus, Shie's collection of wedding blocks continues the tradition today, capturing the sense of the old as well as the innovations of today in the eclectic output from hundreds of her quilting companions around the world.

37. Susan Shie, a contemporary quilter well-known for her Green Quilts project and for her lively and colorful textile works, received blocks from quilters around the world when she married in 1990. Several blocks from her *Wedding Quilt* are shown here. *Joined Hands*; Julie Roseberry; 1990; cotton; 13″ x 12″. (Courtesy Susan Shie)

38. *Mother, Father, Bless Us Dreamers*; Judith Vierow; 1990; batik and embroidery; 13½″ x 14½″. (Courtesy Susan Shie)

39. *Balance*; Rebecca Glass; 1990; mixed media; 38″ x 41″. (Courtesy Susan Shie)

40. *Love Dance*; Tammy Lavanty; 1990; mixed media; 21″ x 21″. (Courtesy Susan Shie)

41. Detail—Chimney Sweep; various makers; Cooperstown area, New York; c. 1859; pieced cotton; 78¼″ x 75½″. (Collection of New York State Historical Association, Cooperstown, New York) Chimney Sweep (sometimes known as Christian Cross) was one of the favored patterns for signature quilts in the mid-nineteenth century. The white cross in the center was ideal for signing a name or inscribing a brief sentiment to the quilt's owner. Although blocks were often made by the signees, it was not unusual for one person to make all the blocks and then have friends and relatives sign them before presentation to the recipient. In some cases, a woman might have collected her friends' signatures before leaving her home for new frontiers and spent part of her time on the trail completing the blocks and sewing them together. Unless family lore or a diary or letter documenting the making accompanies a quilt, it is almost impossible today to know whether such a quilt is actually the handiwork of one or many. Sewing may not always be a clue, as most women of the time were, by necessity, excellent seamstresses.

Friendship's Due

"When this you spy remember I"
—Clara Willson Coleman's Album Quilt, 1862

"Remember well and bear in mind
A constant friend is hard to find
And when you find one that proves true
Change not the old one for the new."

"Change may come and we may part
But distance cannot change the heart
Give to friendship friendship's due
Remember me and I will you."
—Friendship Quilt, Rochester area, 1868

"When you are making a friendship quilt you
are declaring love and faithfulness in the face
of parting, perhaps forever.
Say it with your hands.
Then wave goodbye."[1]

The high value placed during the nineteenth century on emotion and sentiment as part of a woman's moral character was reflected in women's relationships to each other and in their quilts. Although women had always been mutually supportive, bound to each other through shared experiences such as childbirth and always ready to offer help with onerous chores—for sooner or later the help would be amply repaid through in-kind contributions—the growth of an idealized concept of friendship that had started in the late eighteenth century further emphasized this relationship and encouraged even closer female bonding.

Around 1840 a new type of quilt began to be seen, one that carried signatures, often along with short verses or sayings. These came to be known as Friendship, Album, or Signature quilts and eventually were made for almost any occasion that called for an expression of friendship and caring. Friendship quilt designs ranged from the prosaic to the sublime, although most had more sentimental than artistic value. One popular book of the time noted that: "An album quilt is a very pretty idea. A lady gives the size of the square she wishes to each of her lady friends who are willing to contribute to her quilt. They make a square to their own taste, putting a white piece in the center on which they write their own name. Every lady's autograph adorns her own square."[2]

A contemporary description that describes the making of a Friendship quilt and the comparative newness of the form at the time was included in letters written by Abner Wilcox, who, with his wife Lucy, had left New England in 1836 to be missionaries in Hawaii. In 1850, when Wilcox returned home for a lengthy stay due to the need for an operation for one of their children, he wrote to Lucy: "…Louisa [Lucy's sister] is quite busy with a very curious bed-quilt for you…made up of squares given by one and another with their names written on them. You are not forgotten, you may depend…." And later: "July 25th…I today got a letter from Louisa. She writes that she has got our Album quilt on the frame, the one which our Sisters in Norfolk and the ladies were preparing to send you. One and another furnished a square with the name and sometimes a sentiment written in the square. Louisa I believe is taking the brunt of the work….She says that some call it the most splendid thing of the kind ever made in Norfolk…."[3] Abner returned to their home in Waioli with the finished quilt, which used Chimney Sweep blocks set on point.

The number of signatures that appeared on these quilts was rarely a good indication of those who actually sat and stitched. Sometimes one woman would create her own blocks, gather the signatures of her friends on them much as she would have them sign an autograph book, and then join and bind the quilt, perhaps alone, perhaps with several of those who had signed the blocks. At other times, a group of friends or relatives would each contribute blocks, sometimes of their own design and sometimes done to a designated pattern; these might then be quilted at a bee or the blocks would be presented and the receiver herself would join them at some later time.

Many of the elegant Baltimore Albums, most of which

42. Chimney Sweep; makers unknown; New Baltimore, New York; 1847; pieced and appliquéd cotton; size unavailable. (Collection of The Brooklyn Museum, Brooklyn, New York; Gift of Margaret S. Bedell) This Friendship quilt, mentioned in a classic book on quilts, *Old Quilts* (1946) by Dr. William Rush Dunton, Jr., carries the inscription "Miss Caroline A. Trebor's Album Quilt, pieced in the year 1847, New Balto., Green Co, NY." Whether Caroline Trebor pieced all the blocks herself and then collected her friends' signatures, or whether the blocks were made by others and presented to her is unclear, but the quilt is an excellent example of its type and fits well into the popular mode of Chimney Sweep Album quilts. A nice touch that helps to take this quilt out of the ordinary is the addition of a delicate leafy border.

were made as presentation gifts or friendship tokens, are now thought to be the handiwork of women such as Mary Evans or Achsah Goodwin Wilkins, superlative sewers and designers who probably created commissioned blocks, if not entire quilts, for well-to-do ladies of Baltimore who would then sign their names to the blocks.[4] Even the signatures might not be the actual ones of the makers, for in many cases the person with the best penmanship was asked to sign all the names—whether or not that person had actually participated in the making of the quilt.[5] Some of the blocks in the more elaborate album quilts carry no signatures even though they are known to have been made by different people; whether this is because the makers did not want to detract from their design or because it was assumed that the block carried its own message of remembrance to the recipient is not known. The possibilities were many, and every quilt has its own story.

Friendship quilts were at their height of popularity from 1840 to around 1875. Two things likely spurred their development and rapid spread—the fad that started in the 1820s for "annuals" or "albums," small books that were sold as New Year's presents in which friends could inscribe good wishes, poems, and drawings, and the development in the 1830s of noncorrosive indelible ink, which allowed sentiments to be expressed on fabric without deteriorating the cloth.[6] The album concept lent itself well to translation to quilts, and these books are thought to have provided the inspiration for many of the sayings and designs that were so popular just a few years later on the quilts. Sayings and verses such as "Friendship's Offering" and "When I am dead and in my grave/When all my bones are rotten/ When this you see/ remember me/ That I may not be forgotten" were widespread sentiments that appeared on both forms. Katzenberg, in fact, refers to autograph albums and Album quilts as "twin amateur arts" because of their many common elements.[7] Inscriptions in both the album books and quilts followed similar formats, all executed in the best Victorian calligraphy—a sentimental verse or biblical passage, the signature of the well-wisher, a date, and often an elaborate little drawing to accompany the message.[8] Decorative stamps and stencils were also used extensively for embellishment, and a popular type allowed space within the stenciled or stamped design for the signer to inscribe her or his name.

It seemed as though almost any occasion could inspire a Friendship quilt, from leavetakings to weddings, to births, to birthdays and anniversaries, to family reunions, to deaths. Freedom quilts were one special type of Friendship quilt, a type made for young men to mark their coming of age. In the early years of this country, young boys were often apprenticed to skilled craftsmen or professionals in order to learn trades or occupations. Beyond the opportunity to gain a skill or a profession, an apprenticeship usually gave the boy little more than room and board, and life for the duration might involve much work and little play. Boys would be bound out for a period of four to seven years, often remaining with their apprentice master until the age of twenty-one, which was viewed as the legal attainment of adulthood. At that point, the boy would take on the mantle of a man and be free to seek his own way in life, as well as earn money for his work. Finley notes, "No longer could [a boy's] parents or guardian bind him out as an apprentice, take his wages, make him work at home for nothing or legally restrain his actions in any way. He was *free*."[9] This critical turning point in life was sometimes marked by a celebration or

43. Album; Mrs. Eldad Miller and others; Cross River, New York; c. 1861; pieced, appliquéd, and embroidered cotton and silks with stuffed work; 90″ x 75″. Photograph by Helga Photo Studio. (Collection of Museum of American Folk Art, New York City; Gift of Dr. Stanley and Jacqueline Schneider, 1980.8.1.) Makers with varying degrees of skill contributed their blocks to this quilt, and one of the most amusing is the block showing two red stockings and green button shoes. The elegant basket of fruit in the first row is signed by Mrs. Eldad Miller along with the date, Nov. 1, 1861. Research has shown that the signers ranged in age from fifteen years old (Carrie Silkman) to fifty-six years old (Mrs. Miller, neé Nancy Q. Avery); many of them were related. No clear reason stands out for why the quilt was made. It is possible that the quilt was a patriotic endeavor, intended as a fundraiser, as all the signers were part of a local Ladies Aid Society that raised money for various worthy causes. (For more information see Paula Laverty, "Many Hands: The Story of an Album Quilt," *Folk Art*, Vol. 18, No. 1, Spring 1993, pp. 52-57.)

44. Whole Cloth; Sarah Smith, Hannah Callender, and Catherine Smith; Philadelphia, Pennsylvania; 1761; silk top, wool backing; 101″ x 101″. (Independence National Historic Park Collection, Philadelphia, Pennsylvania; Gift of Mr. and Mrs. Elliston P. Morris) This elegant spread, one of the earliest quilts known to have been specifically made as a Friendship piece, is a testimony to the friendship of three young women, as noted on the quilt itself: "Drawn by Sarah Smith Stiched [sic] by Hannah Callender and Catherine Smith in Testimony of their Friendship 10 mo 5th 1761." The makers are believed to have belonged to influential families in the Quaker community of Philadelphia; the use of silk on the face of the spread seems to indicate that they were well-to-do.

45. Album; makers unknown; New York State; 1840s; pieced and appliquéd cotton; 84″ x 70″. Photograph by Scott Bowron. (Courtesy Judith and James Milne, Inc., New York City) This friendship sampler contains blocks of two sizes, the smaller of which were joined together to match the size of the larger. Each block seems to have been quilted individually by the makers, posing the likely possibility that they were presented separately to the recipient, who then later put them together with sashing and backing.

46. Album; Mary Foster, Elizabeth Holland, and others; possibly East Bloomfield, New York; c. 1845; appliquéd cotton; 99″ x 99″. Information courtesy the New York Quilt Project, Museum of American Folk Art. Photograph by Scott Bowron. (Collection of Paula Zimmerman) Little is known about this beautiful quilt, but it is of the Baltimore Album genre, and it can be assumed that it was made as a token of friendship or respect for a member of the community. Two names can be read in the blocks; others may have faded with time.

other ceremony to acknowledge the boy's new status, and gifts—which could include a quilt made by family and friends—might be presented. Such quilts came to be known as Freedom quilts because they signaled liberation from the bonds of childhood and bound work, and they often included masculine symbols such as eagles, ships, guns, horses, or symbols of fraternal orders that were indicative of the boy's new standing in life.[10]

As opportunities for education and employment expanded in the early part of the nineteenth century, the apprenticeship system began to die away and with it there was a lessening of the ceremonies that took note of a boy's emancipation. The fashion for freedom parties (and quilts) did not totally disappear, however, but its character was somewhat changed. Rather than recognizing freedom from the bonds of apprenticeship, the celebration focused on the coming of age, the boy's independence from his family, and his official status as an adult who might soon have his own family. It is from this latter type of celebration, which developed after about 1825, that the Freedom quilts known today resulted. As has been noted earlier, the quilt that the boy received at this time was often put away, not to be used until he married.

Leavetakings seem to have spurred the making of the greatest number of Friendship quilts, for their period of greatest popularity coincided with the peak of migration to and settlement of the West, when many people, pushed by a growing population and a fluctuating economy, gathered their families and left their former homes to look for opportunity and fortune on the expanding frontier. The women took with them tangible reminders of their former homes and friends—some of whom would never be seen again—in the form of Friendship quilts. Not only were these quilts comforting reminders of their onetime homes, they also served as tangible remembrances of the

47. Album; makers unknown; Illinois; c. 1845; pieced and appliquéd cotton; 82″ x 86″. (Courtesy Laura Fisher/Antique Quilts and Americana, New York City) The purpose of this quilt is underscored by an inked inscription at the top that reads "Friendship's Offering." Each block carries a different signature. Although the patterns are based on familiar and popular designs of the time, some show charming and original deviations.

48. Freedom Quilt; various makers; location unknown; 1886; pieced and embroidered cotton; 81¼″ x 63¾″. (Collection of Los Angeles County Museum of Art, Los Angeles, California; Gift of the Betty Horton Collection) Made as a gift for a young man's coming of age, the inscription on this quilt reads: "Presented to John W Peterson on his Twenty-first birthday May 27 86." The blocks are embroidered with the initials of the makers.

49. Freedom Quilt; made for William M. Ketcham; location unknown; c. 1861; pieced and appliquéd cotton; 90″ x 79″. Photograph courtesy Kelter-Malcé Antiques, New York City. (Private collection) The Bible in the third row of this splendid piece is open to Psalm XXIII, and the following inscription is written below the Bible: "From Mother 1862. My son, hear the instruction of thy Father and forsake not the Law of thy Mother." This Freedom quilt bears many similarities to an earlier one made for Benjamin Almoney of Norrisville, Maryland, on the occasion of his 21st birthday on December 10, 1845, illustrated by Dr. William Rush Dunton, Jr., in his book *Old Quilts*. Both make use of several blocks showing masculine symbols such as an eagle, flags, and an anchor (in the case of Almoney's, a ship), which were commonly used on Freedom quilts. Dunton notes that a party was arranged by Almoney's sisters, and each of the sixteen blocks in his quilt was made by one of the young ladies attending. The blocks were probably later put together and quilted by one of the women in his family, and it is most likely that William Ketcham's mother provided the same service for this quilt.

50. Album; members of the Nicholson, Miller, Biddle, Parrish, Cox, Hay, and Shinn families; Philadelphia, Pennsylvania; 1843; pieced and appliquéd cotton and chintz; 98⅞″ x 97⅞″. (Collection of The Smithsonian Institution, Washington, D.C.; Gift of Mr. and Mrs. Thomas B. Grave) Hannah Nicholson was given this quilt by friends and relatives living in the Philadelphia area. The nineteen-year-old Hannah may have received it either as a going-away present or as a wedding gift or as a combination of the two (she married Howell Grave in Richmond, Indiana). Hannah and the makers and signers of the blocks are assumed to be Quakers as the inscriptions include dates given in the Quaker style, for example, "3rd month 22nd 1843" or "8th month 26th 1843."

51. Detail—Chimney Sweep; makers unknown; Rochester, New York; 1868; pieced cotton; 84¼" x 77½". Photograph courtesy New York Quilt Project, Museum of American Folk Art, New York City. (Collection of Doris Shandell) This quilt provides an ideal example of how the Chimney Sweep pattern lent itself not only to signatures but also to more extensive inscriptions. There are many humorous verses on this quilt, and their content seems to hint that this might have been an engagement gift: "Here I stand/ Tall and straight/ I'll never live/ Without a mate" and "Fall from the housetop & broke your neck/ Fall in the sea from off the deck/ Fall from the twinkling stars above—/ But never, never fall in love!" Another verse reads: "I'm a little man and I have a little wife/ I sometimes think she's the bane of my life." Several of the blocks are addressed to Celia. The last names Beadle and Green appear several times each; there are also references to Celia as "cousin" and "granddaughter," so makers were most likely part of an extended family group. Although many of the inscriptions tie the quilt to the Rochester, New York, area, some blocks have "Michigan" following the name and indicate that several family members were part of the westward migration following the Civil War.

community that was left behind, a record and perpetuation of the bonds of friendship, for the people who signed the quilt symbolically stayed together. Many of the sayings penned on Friendship quilts admonish the recipient to "remember me/ when this you see"—a hope, perhaps, that time, distance, and a new way of life would not be sufficient to break the ties to the old.

These closeknit bonds and the interdependence of women made change a wrenching experience for the nineteenth-century woman. Life on the frontier was particularly difficult in this respect; for every woman who went West to meet the unknown with enthusiasm and optimism, there were many more who went with reluctance to leave the safe and the known, regardless of

the opportunities envisioned elsewhere. Once in their new homes, which often initially were of the most primitive or makeshift types, they would frequently be cut off from the easy companionship of other women; distances between homes were great and transportation limited, making visiting difficult. Many diaries lament the lack of female companionship, and the loss of regular interaction with close friends and relatives was keenly felt:

> Nothing can atone for the loss of the society of friends....[11]

> We do not see a woman at all. All men, single or batchelors, and one gets tired of them.[12]

> O Martha, what I would give to see you now....I miss you more than I can find words to express....[13]

The need to establish new ties was strong, and as soon as was feasible after settlement, women would go to great effort to find other women with whom to share their friendship, their feelings, and their work. Proximity often dictated friendships (although proximity on the frontier might still mean sizeable distances between homes), and when they were able to meet with other women, their visits might be prolonged, as the following description indicates, because the opportunity might not be repeated again for several months:

> Sutter engaged my husband...to be blacksmith for the sawmill....Myself to cook for the hands which were about 15 men....After a while...I wanted to see a white woman again so they took me and my child about 15 miles to...see Mrs. Wimmer & her family. I stayed two days & nights & then returned home... she was very glad to see me and we did not sleep very much, but put in the time talking while I stayed....[14]

Those women who took their quilts with them to the frontier took more than decoration for their new homes; they carried with them mementoes of home and friends, of shared companionship and shared chores.[15] The quilts were tangible embodiments of the work and skills of, often, all the women in a community, its dense web made explicit in the signatures. The quilts provided a needed sense of continuity at a time when life must often have seemed chaotic and hostile. They were important ties to the past, and it is for this reason that many Friendship quilts have been preserved so carefully through the years. That sentiment rather than function was the keynote in these quilts is underscored by the fact that many Friendship pieces known today are tops only and were never backed or quilted.

Friendship quilts varied tremendously, from quickly pieced repetitive blocks with a white space in each for a signature to the very elaborate and highly crafted Album type. Certain patterns became particular favorites for the

52. Crazy; Florence Barton Loring, Olive Frances Barton, Mrs. Isaac Atwater, Julia Estes, Mrs. Loren Fletcher, and others; Minneapolis, Minnesota; c. 1905; pieced, appliquéd, and embroidered silk, satin, ribbons, and embroidery materials; 77″ x 65″. (Collection of Minneapolis Institute of the Arts, Minneapolis, Minnesota; Gift of Eleanor Atwater, Martha Atwater, Sandra Butler, Ellie Donovan, Suzanne H. Hodder, Anita Kunin, Laura Miles, Eleanor W. Reid, and Kathleen Scott) The women who made the blocks in this quilt as an expression of their friendship were all leaders of Minneapolis society at the turn of the century. They reflected their pride in their families, their interests, their favorite organizations, and their pets in the popular Crazy format of the time. A Red Cross, musical notations (from Beethoven's Ninth Symphony and Schumann's Quintet), an Egyptian scene, an American flag, a picture of James Gillespie Blaine (a U.S. Senator and Secretary of State from Minnesota), and a DAR button are only a few of the many symbols found on this quilt. Florence Barton Loring, who assembled the many blocks, was the wife of Charles Loring, known as the "father" of the Minneapolis Park system.

repetitive blocks and were especially well suited to this use—Chimney Sweep (also known as Christian Cross, when used by church groups, and Friendship Block) and Fleur-de lis being among them. There were some early regional differences, with the single-pattern style being favored in the Northeast (this type was especially popular among Quaker groups, who had a particular affinity for Signature quilts[16]) and the Album in the Midatlantic and South, but by late in the century all types were being made throughout the country, the style depending only on the whim of the makers. Even the Crazy-quilt format was adapted to use for Friendship quilts in the latter part of the nineteenth century.

Although Friendship quilts declined somewhat in popularity as the rush to the frontier subsided, they continued to be made for all the other occasions noted earlier, or simply as an excuse to express friendship. They were also strongly favored by church groups, schools, societies, and similar institutional groups, especially in the form of presentation pieces. As such, they not only allowed for a tribute to a respected minister, teacher, community leader, or outstanding society member but also provided a way to record and memorialize the existence of the group.

Friendship quilts continue to be made today. In some cases, the motivation remains the same as in preceding years—to mark rites of passage from one life stage to another or a move to a different community—but more often they are made as a spontaneous voicing in fabric of the pleasure of sharing and in one another's company. Sometimes these are made in the traditional style of Friendship and Album quilts, complete with signatures and carefully crafted verses and sayings; other times they are simply quilts put together by a group of women for one of their own. Whatever the reason and the style, there is no question that they are as welcome by the recipient today as they were in past times, and they carry the same quiet messages, not only to "Remember Me" but also "You are not forgotten."

53. Crown of Thorns; Ethel Johnson Stetler and members of her crochet club; New Cristobal, Canal Zone; c. 1934; pieced cotton; 82½″ x 66″. (Courtesy The Oakland Museum History Department, Acc. # H92.44.2, Oakland, California) This pretty quilt was made for Elizabeth A. Stetler by her mother Ethel and members of Ethel's crochet club when Elizabeth left the Canal Zone to attend college. Elizabeth, who had never before been out of Panama (her father was an engineer who worked in the Canal Zone), chose Stanford University in California, because, she said, she wanted to see more of the world. However, the girl, reared in the tropical warmth of the Canal Zone and unused to the more temperate climate of the north, did not find the quilt enough to keep her warm during the Palo Alto winters and had to buy blankets as well!

54. The Cathy Quilt; made by friends of Cathy Rasmussen; New York City and environs; 1992; pieced cottons, cotton blends; 95½″ x 73½″. Photograph by Karen Bell. (Collection of Cathy Rasmussen) A contemporary version of the traditional signature quilt, many friends contributed blocks and helped in the tieing of this lively quilt, made as an expression of friendship and caring at a time when the recipient was ill. The Star pattern and block size were chosen by the quilt's organizers, but participants were free to choose their own fabrics within the organizing theme of purple—the recipient's favorite color. Some blocks contain only the signature of the maker, while others carry the names of several people who may have worked on the quilt in different ways. In the best friendship tradition, several blocks include verses, and an ancient Chinese poem of friendship has been inscribed on a block on the back of the quilt: "I want to be your friend/ Forever and ever without break or decay./ When the hills are all flat/ And the rivers are all dry,/ When it lightens and thunders in winter,/ When it rains and snows in summer,/ When Heaven and Earth mingle—/Not til then will I part from you."

55a. Detail of the Fleur-de-Lis quilt illustrated in figure 55; Amherst, New York; 1849.

A Symbol of Respect and Admiration

"Back around 1850 there seems to have been a fashion of making quilts of
an unusual character for presentation to some favored man or woman,
often a clergyman. It was natural for the ladies of the congregation to
show their regard by making a quilt to commemorate his incumbency."[1]

"This quilt is but a symbol
Of respect and admiration
To our pastor and his wife
From friends and congregation."
—From the presentation quilt for
Reverend and Mrs. L.C. Mattoon

"Pastor Williams...was a big person in our lives....Well, Mrs. Wilcox got
the idea to put up a quilt for him....We outdid ourselves appliquéing each
one of us a block."[2]

Along with their responsibilities for home and family,
women frequently took on the mantle of caretaker of
history and ceremony for their communities. As such,
they were the ones who helped to make visible the
relationships and connections between important local
(and sometimes national) figures and institutions and the
community. Often these connections were recognized
symbolically through the presentation of a quilt. Within
this context, quilts can be viewed as ritual or ceremonial
objects that serve to represent and acknowledge the ties,
affiliations, and obligations of an individual to the
community. They act as a tangible reminder to the
recipient of his or her explicit linkages to a specific
population and of the bonds that have been forged
together through work in common or shared goals. And,
in their creation, the quilts also served to further
strengthen the bonds between the members of the
presenting group.

These quilts, known as Presentation quilts, are similar to
Friendship quilts but usually reflect a greater degree of
formality in concept if not always in design. They were
made specifically as tokens of esteem for well-respected
persons in the community, testimonials to those who often
had had a major influence on the lives of the community
members. Pastors, doctors, leaders of fraternal and
sororal orders or societies, or teachers—all of whom held
special places of regard and respect within a community—were frequently recipients on a local level, but
quilts were made and presented to leading political and
popular figures as well. The quilts usually were presented
to mark some significant stage of the person's life—
retirement, departure for another position, marriage, or,
occasionally, the birth of a child—or a major event such as
a centennial celebration or other significant anniversary

of the institution with which the individual was affiliated.
Sometimes, however, they were made simply to reflect
the esteem in which the honoree was held, a special
expression of appreciation from a grateful congregation
or community. And, like Friendship quilts, they also
embodied a material reminder of the group, an insurance
that just as they appreciated the individual, so too would
the receiver continue to appreciate them in the future use
of the quilt.

Like many Friendship quilts, Presentation quilts usually
were the product of a group effort, a lasting gift that
recognized the interaction between the recipient and the
group's members and a tribute to the contribution of the
individual to the group or to the community at large. They
grew out of the group's awareness of the value of the
person to the community and reflected the communal
commitment to a visible and public observance of that
value. They were functional gifts at a time when bedding
was still counted among the household goods of some
worth (wills often stipulated the value and distribution of
various items of bedding until well into the nineteenth
century), as well as being decorative; they also encom-
passed the symbolic merit of the time and effort that was
devoted to their creation.

These quilts were often far more elaborate in design
than many Friendship quilts, as the women making them
wanted their gift to stand out, to be appreciated
aesthetically as well as for the sentiment it represented.
The fine work and care that went into its production was
a reflection of the regard that the quilt embodied for the
recipient and, in essence, it became a showcase for the
creative ability of the presenting community. The more
elaborate of the Presentation quilts featured either elegant
pieced and appliquéd coordinated designs that indicate

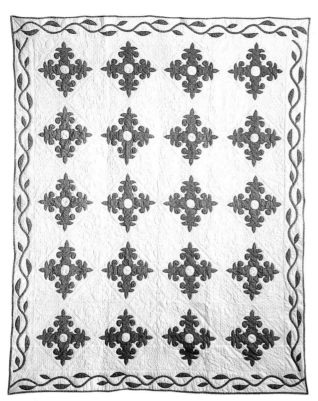

55. Fleur-de-Lis; makers probably members of the Reformed Mennonites; Amherst, New York; 1849; appliquéd cotton; 83″ x 68″. Photograph by Scott Bowron courtesy New York Quilt Project, Museum of American Folk Art, New York City. (Collection of Warren H. Miller) This Signature quilt was the product of a group of Mennonite women, and the wealth of elegant quilting in the plain blocks reflects the tradition for which Mennonite quilters are still respected today. The quilt was most likely made as a presentation gift. It was in the family of Mary Snearly, one of the signers, until 1962. Her father was a minister of the Reformed Mennonite Congregation in the Erie County area at the time the quilt was made, and he would have been a logical recipient for this token of his congregation's affection.

56. Floral; Ladies of the Chanceford Congregation; possibly Pennsylvania; 1850–1860; appliquéd cotton; 102″ x 100″. Photograph by Scott Bowron courtesy Susan Parrish Antiques, New York City. The center block of this elegant quilt is inscribed "A Donation to/ the Rev John Farquhar./ From the Ladies of/ Chanceford Congregation." Whether "donation" is to be taken literally is not clear; perhaps the ladies intended the quilt to be simply a token of their esteem—and the exquisite work in it might point to that interpretation—or perhaps it was intended to be sold, raffled, or auctioned by the minister for the benefit of the church.

57. Album; members of the Wallingford branch of the Oneida Community; Wallingford, Connecticut; 1873; pieced, embroidered, and appliquéd cotton; 89½″ x 79″. (Collection of the Oneida Community Mansion House, Wallingford, Connecticut) Inspired by Harriet Holton Noyes, wife of John Humphrey Noyes, the founder of the Oneida Community, Community members in Oneida, New York, and Wallingford, Connecticut, produced over one hundred quilt blocks. The blocks judged to be the best were put into a quilt presented to Mother Noyes, and the remaining blocks, stitched together into the one shown here, became known as the "second-best" quilt, which was most likely also presented to Mother Noyes. The blocks cover a wide spectrum of design, from ones showing Community occupations and interests, to popular patterns of the day, to those with a more personal meaning that is lost today. The *OC Circular* of March 24, 1873, noted that "there are besides various designs taken from carpets, paper-hangings, oil-clothes, stoles, etc., to which we can give no name.... It is an album bed-quilt with the wildest variations, and we imagine that half a century hence it will be an interesting memorial of the industries and aspirations of the year 1873."

58. Harriet Holton Noyes
("Mother" Noyes), c. 1860s.

59. Cory Presentation Album; members of the Presbyterian Church; Perth Amboy, New Jersey; 1852–1853; appliquéd cotton; 93″ x 93½″. Photograph by Ken Burris. (Collection of Shelburne Museum, Shelburne, Vermont; Gift of Walter Kiggins) This elegant quilt was presented to Reverend Cory of the Perth Amboy Presbyterian Church on the occasion of his retirement after twenty years of ministry there. One hundred and twenty-one of his parishioners joined together to create this lovely quilt. Each block is signed, many are dated, and many also contain either a biblical passage or a verse from the psalms.

60. Album; Ladies of the Presbyterian Church; Maltaville, New York; 1847; appliquéd cotton with embroidery; 92¼″ x 91¼″. (Collection of The Smithsonian Institution, Washington, D.C.; Gift of Mrs. Isaac Carrington Morton) The center block of this quilt contains a poem of friendship and an inscription, "Presented to Mrs. Mary B Hill/ As an expression of esteem/ by the ladies of Malta Ville/ Malta Ville April 1847." Mary Benton Barnard Hill was the wife of the Reverend William Hill, the pastor of the Maltaville church. Although the reason for the presentation is unknown, Mrs. Hill clearly was held in great affection by her husband's parishioners and it is likely that this quilt was made as a pure expression of friendship and love. The blocks are signed by nearly sixty women, and some of them have included their own verses to add a more personal note to the quilt: "A richer gift earth ne'er bestowes/ Than a heart where friendship glows" (Mrs. Emily Jordan); "This though a trifle take/ And keep it for the donor's sake" (Mrs. Phebe A. Cox). The quilt is a compendium of popular designs of the time, although some seem to be unique, such as the block showing Saturn and its rings. One block is a rebus: "CROSS on earth CROWN in heaven."

61. Presentation Sampler; students at Sunnyside School; Darke Co., Ohio; 1894; pieced and appliquéd cottons; 90″ x 66″. (Private collection) This lively and eccentric quilt was apparently made as a presentation gift for a teacher (thought to be Eli Hoke, whose name appears on the quilt); the inscription reads: "Accept our valued friendship,/ And roll it up in cotton,/ And think it not illusion/ Because so easily gotten." Although the date appears to be 1814, a close examination shows that some threads forming a part of the "9" in the date of "1894" have been lost. Several quilts or quilt tops made between 1892 and 1915 are known that bear a great similarity to this one in pattern, color, and style; they were made to celebrate special occasions such as marriages and birthdays and all have been found in the counties of Darke, Miami, and Montgomery in Ohio. Research has shown that "Sunnyside" is not a town but a one-room country schoolhouse in this three-county area. (My thanks to Sue C. Cummings for sharing the results of her ongoing research on this and similar Ohio quilts.)

that the group who made it agreed on the pattern together or a lively assortment of appliquéd Album-type blocks (of which there are many excellent examples out of the Baltimore Album tradition), each produced by a different member of the group and designed to her own tastes (or, in the case of a number of the Baltimore quilts, blocks commissioned by ladies in the group and then executed by others).[3] Sometimes the quilt would be bound and quilted by the group, but occasionally the completed blocks alone would be given, to be finished at a later time by the recipient (or, as was usually the case when the individual was a man, by his wife).

Presentation quilts might not carry the names of all who had worked on them. Although occasional ones are seen in which each block is signed or initialed, many others carry only the names of the recipient(s), perhaps followed by an inclusive statement of contributors, such as "From your grateful students," "From the loving members of your congregation," or "Presented by the Ladies Aid Society."

Still others carry no overt notice at all of the presenters or the receiver, and it is oral or written family histories alone that today provide us with the information on the original purpose of the quilt. For Presentation quilts, the individuals involved in their making were less important than the concept of the group as a whole; the full meaning of the quilt was embodied in the idea of *community* both in the presentation and in the commitment to acknowledging and honoring the recipient.

As indicated by Dunton in the opening quote above, Presentation quilts in the nineteenth and into the early twentieth centuries seem to have most often been church-related. This should not be surprising, given the importance of religion and the presence of the church in the restricted lives of many nineteenth-century women. The ladies of a congregation would frequently honor their minister or his wife with a quilt, especially at the end of an appointment or when this minister retired; missionaries about to embark on foreign journeys replete with

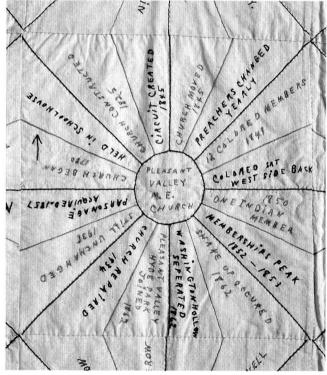

62, 62a. Signature; made by members of the Pleasant Valley Methodist Episcopal Church; Pleasant Valley, New York; c. 1938; embroidered cotton and muslin; 80″ x 66″. Photograph by Scott Bowron courtesy New York Quilt Project, Museum of American Folk Art, New York City. (Collection of Jacqueline M. and Edward G. Atkins) This simple Signature quilt was made as a presentation gift for Florence Phinney, wife of Reverend W.R. Phinney who served several churches in the Poughkeepsie, New York, area in the 1930s. A type of quilt that was often used for fundraising, it might have been used for this purpose prior to its presentation to Mrs. Phinney, a minister in her own right. The quilt contains well over 600 names and these were embroidered by many different hands. One of the blocks encapsulates the history of the church from its establishment in 1780 through 1938 (see detail, fig. 62a).

63. Album; ladies of the West New Hempstead Reformed Church; Spring Valley, New York; c. 1862; pieced and appliquéd cotton; 81" x 88". Photograph by Scott Bowron courtesy New York Quilt Project, Museum of American Folk Art, New York City. (Collection of the West New Hempstead Reformed Church) This glorious Album quilt was made for the Reverend Peter Allen and presented to him at the end of his twenty-five-year tenure at the West New Hempstead Reformed Church. After remaining in his family for many years, the quilt was then donated to the church, where it holds a place of pride and reflects a bit of its history—the original church building may be seen in one of the blocks. The names of the quiltmakers are inscribed on the blocks and give clear evidence of their skills with the needle.

64. Wagon Wheel; various makers; Humphrey, New York; 1859; pieced and appliquéd cotton. 81″ x 66¼″. Information and photograph (by Scott Bowron) courtesy New York Quilt Project, Museum of American Folk Art, New York City. (Collection of Miriam and Ivan E. Hayes) The Reverend Russell Draper Hays, along with the Reverend Samuel W. Titus and William Storrs, organized the First Baptist Church of Humphrey in 1845. This lovely, carefully executed quilt was made for Reverend Hayes and his wife by devoted friends who may also have been members of that church's congregation. An inscription in the border of the quilt reads: "A token of friendship presented to Mr. and Mrs. R.D. Hays by those whose names are upon it. Completed Nov. 12, 1859." A list of twenty-four names—women and men—follows, with their towns (all were from Humphrey or nearby Ischua and Hinsdale) noted after the name.

64a. Reverend Russell Draper Hays

64b. Jane Havens Little Hays
(Mrs. Russell Draper Hays)

65. Fleur-de-Lis; friends of Ellen Calder; Harrisburg, Pennsylvania; 1851; appliquéd cotton; 85¾" x 84⅞". (Collection of The Smithsonian Institution, Washington, D.C.; Gift of Mrs. Laura Calder Stonebreaker) Ellen Winebrenner Calder, married to the Reverend James K. Calder, received this quilt from her friends when she and her husband were about to leave Harrisburg to do missionary work in China. Some of the blocks carry inked religious inscriptions or verses in addition to the names of her friends: "When on a bounding wave,/ or in a Heathen land,/ May God in Mercy Save,/ And guide you by the hand./ And when your labors cease,/ And you no more must roam,/ May you return in peace,/ To your beloved home." (Malvina L. Ingram); "Rejoice and be exceedingly glad, for great is Your reward in Heaven" (R. H. Clerickson [?]); "Jesus Christ the same yesterday and today and forever" (Julia A. Emerson). The Fleur-de-Lis pattern is often used by religious groups for presentation pieces.

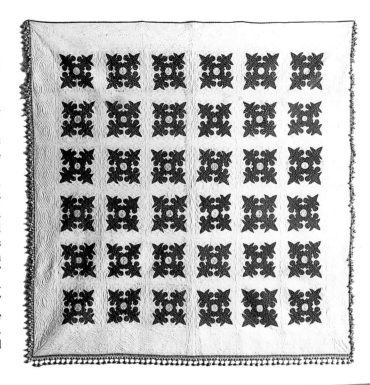

66. Bible Verse Quilt; ladies of the West Chazy Wesleyan Church; West Chazy, New York; c. 1939; pieced and embroidered cotton; 92" x 69". Information and photograph (by Scott Bowron) courtesy New York Quilt Project, Museum of American Folk Art, New York City. (Collection of Betty LaPlante) This simple quilt, with each square embroidered with a verse from the Bible, was made for the Reverend L.C. Mattoon and his wife to mark his tenure at the West Chazy Church from 1929 to 1939. The ladies of the church seemed to have had a good time working on this quilt, and one of them composed a poem, entitled "Tale of the Quilt." In it, she relates that the group wanted to surprise the pastor, but one day, as the quilt was being finished at one of the ladies' homes, he and his wife almost walked in on the quilting bee! The hostess quickly bundled the quilters into another room as the Mattoons approached her door, and she then entertained the unsuspecting couple as the other women held in their laughter and continued to sew in the next room. The poem, presented along with the quilt, ends: "This quilt is but a symbol/ Of respect and admiration/ To our pastor and his wife/ From friends and congregation."

unknown hazards were also so honored, the quilts serving both as testimonials to the zeal of the sponsoring society as well as recognition of the need for some basic necessities (such as bedding) in their new and often difficult life style. Women and men within the local church group might also be honored for their dedication and zeal in, respectively, heading the ladies'-aid or sewing societies or promoting the goals of the church. Although not always originally intended as such, a quilt made for raffle or auction might sometimes end up as a Presentation quilt. The winner or purchaser of the quilt might choose to present it back to the leader of the group that made it in honor of a job well done, and several such examples are known.

Church-related Presentation quilts might depict popular patterns of the day, but they also frequently incorporated biblical verses or other religious sayings, especially when the quilt was to be presented to a pastor or Sunday school teacher. In this way, the quilt also served to reaffirm what the community had gained from the

person honored. Occasionally, a representation of the church itself was included on the quilt, perhaps as a keepsake for the recipient. Some of these quilts also served a dual purpose—that of a subscription fundraiser as well as a testimonial. Church members would pay to have their names inscribed on the quilt in thread or ink, and the finished product would then be presented to the minister (or his wife). This diary entry reflects the making of one such quilt as well as giving some insight into the time and number of people involved in the final work on it:

15th Tues	Afternoon I went around the neighborhood and got the rest of the subscription for Mrs. R quilt & invited the quilters thursday and friday
16th Wed	Ma Mrs Fisk Mrs Philips worked all day to get the quilt ready to quilt
17th Thur	9 quilters here to day
18th Frid	7 quilters here
19th Sat	6 quilters here we got it off...
21st Mon	Emeline and I finished the quilt & presented to the Eld's wife.[4]

Occasionally the money raised as a result of the quilt subscription would be given to the recipient along with the quilt, but it might also be channeled into whatever special project was being financed by the ladies'-aid group at the moment.

Sometimes a Presentation quilt was made in secrecy and presented as a surprise (as in the Piety quilt shown here). Other times, the recipient might have been active in the creation of the quilt, as is the case with those quilts that were auctioned and then presented to a key participant in

67. Detail—Sampler; members of the Methodist Church Circle; Tyre, New York; 1850–1851; appliquéd cotton; 97″ x 86½″. Information and photograph courtesy New York Quilt Project, Museum of American Folk Art, New York City. (Collection of Virginia Jamieson) Each of these blocks was made by a different church member, and the designs are as varied as the names. Several of the blocks show tools or other implements, and it is thought that these represent the employment of the husband of the woman responsible for that block. Each block was quilted separately, then they were joined and presented to the wife of the minister of the Tyre Methodist Church. Although the color and style of the quilt might lead one to believe that it had been made in a later period, some of the blocks are dated and others show substantial wear, so the mid-nineteenth-century date seems justified.

68, 69. Bicentennial; eighth-grade students, Glandorf Elementary School; Ottawa, Ohio; 1976; embroidered cotton with hand painting; 109″ x 73″. (Collection of the Gerald R. Ford Museum, Grand Rapids, Michigan) The students in a U.S. History class put their studies to work in this bright quilt that touches on some highlights—and sidelights—of this country's history. The blocks, designed by history teacher Ken Heath and made by his students, are handpainted and outlined in chain-stitch embroidery. The central eagle and the red, white, and blue binding carry through the Bicentennial theme. The quilt was presented by the class to President Ford during a ceremony in the White House Rose Garden on April 12, 1976, as seen in the accompanying photograph, figure 69.

the fundraising project, or he or she might have played a more passive role, as is shown in this example:

Pastor Williams...was a big person in our lives—the traveling Methodist preacher....Well, Mrs. Wilcox got the idea to put up a quilt for him. Something special...we outdid ourselves appliquéing each one of us a block. And we sent out the word by him along the circuit for ladies of other congregations to send a design for the top; he would carry them little appliquéd pieces easy in the saddlebags, no weight to 'em. We gathered it all in and put that quilt together. That was a feat in those days. He said he never seen anything so pretty. It was a treasure.[5]

Today, Presentation quilts are still being made by groups, and much of the same motivation lies behind them—the desire to give recognition in a lasting and tangible way, to create a concrete statement of the recipient's impact on the group, and to reinforce or create enduring bonds between the recipient to the group. Yet other motivations may also sometimes play a part, and quilts may often be presented to public figures as a means

of increasing social awareness of certain issues or events. Although ministers, doctors, teachers, and other local figures may still receive their share of homage today for all the traditional reasons, many of the people honored with Presentation quilts are more likely to be nationally known, people with whom few, if any, of the contributors to a quilt have had any personal acquaintance.

Presidents, senators, and other members of Congress and their spouses have received many quilts from well-wishers, some given simply out of love and respect for the office, others to acknowledge or commemorate some action or event that occurred during the incumbent's time in office. The 1976 Bicentennial, for example, was an event that spurred the creation of numerous quilts to President and Mrs. Ford. Other national figures are likewise often the recipients of a group's desire to acknowledge their contribution to society. Several quilts created by the On-Line Quilters Guild were presented to General Norman Schwartzkopf in recognition of his role in the Gulf War (see fig. 112), and several groups have given recognition to leaders and historic figures in the Civil Rights movement, including one made in honor of

Rosa Parks by the Boise Peace Project (see fig. 96), and others made to commemorate Harriet Tubman and Frederick Douglass by the Negro History Club in California.[6]

In some instances, the quilt recipient is an entity, rather than a person, as is the case with the Album quilt that was done for a regional division of the New York State Power Authority; others have been presented to civic or social groups that are thought to have contributed in some significant way to the cultural, economic, or social well-being of the presenting community. At times, the intent may be to leave behind a permanent reminder of the presenting group, a memorialization, as it were, of the ties of those within the group to each other and to the receiving institution, as with the quilt created by an eighth-grade graduating class as a presentation gift to their school.

Whatever form they may take today, and to whomever they may be given, Presentation quilts remain a living part of the American heritage in quilts. Whether a presentation piece grows out of the ongoing and consistent activities of a group as a gift for one of its own, or whether the group comes together only on a short-term basis in order to create a quilt for a specific person or event, each participant has contributed her piece to the whole, and the whole will stand as much a tribute and commendation of their work together as to the ostensible reason for its creation.

70. Power Authority Album; quilters in the Marcy South power district; New York State; pieced, appliquéd, and embroidered cotton blends; 77½" x 55". (Collection of New York State Museum, Albany, New York) Local quilters in participating townships decided to commemorate the establishment of this power district with this lively quilt. Each quilter picked some facet of her township to represent; some picked historical themes, others verged on the controversial, as the one that shows transmission lines running through an otherwise scenic countryside.

71. "Where It's O.K. To Go Out Of The Lines"; eighth-grade students at The Center School; New York, New York; 1992; pieced and appliquéd cotton, synthetics, lamé, sequins, plastic, other mixed media; 84″ x 72″. Photograph by Karen Bell. (Collection of The Center School) Paula Nadelstern, a professional quilter, inspired members of her daughter's eighth-grade class to create a quilt as a presentation gift to their school when their class graduated. Each child in the class participated, although some had never sewn before. The children were free to give full range to their imagination, as long as the block related in some way to the school. The final results ranged from the whimsical—"The Attack of the Sex Education Eggs"; to down to earth— the block showing the graffiti on the walls of the girls' rest room; to contemplative—the block showing the cycle of seed to flower. Elaine Schwartz, principal of the school, notes that producing the quilt was an experience that taught more than sewing skills, as cooperation and coordination were other pieces of the lesson learned in its making.

72. Crazy; students at Soule College; Murfreesboro, Tennessee; 1891; pieced, appliquéd, and embroidered wool, velvet, cotton; 74″ x 71½″. Photograph courtesy Tennessee Quilt Project, Chattanooga, Tennessee. (Collection of Jeanne Gilmore Webb) Soule College, in operation from 1851 to 1917, was a well-known boarding school for girls. It had high standards, and subjects ranging from science and mathematics through languages, music, art, and needlework were taught. This quilt, characteristic in design of the time, was made by the students as a gift to J.N. Holt, an itinerant Cumberland Presbyterian preacher in the Rutherford County area. Both his name and his wife's initials— S.L.S., for Susan L. Smotherman—appear on the quilt, along with the year (which is repeated five times).

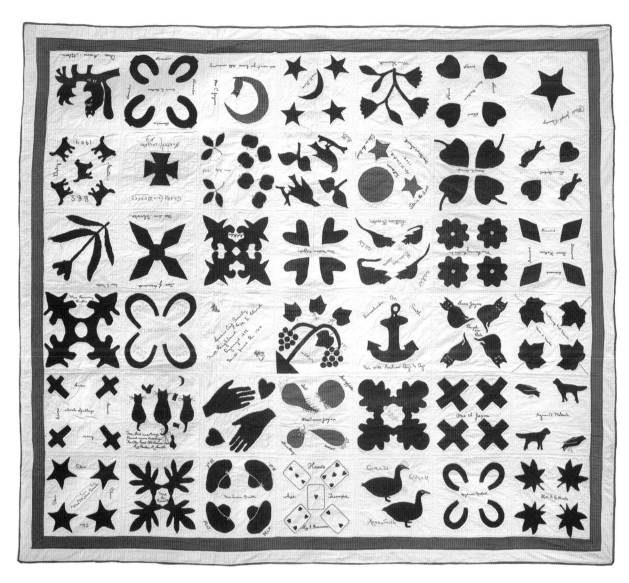

73. Eccentric Sampler; Ladies Aid Society of North Highlands Methodist Episcopal Church; Phillipstown, New York; 1904; appliquéd cotton; 82″ x 73″. Information and photograph (by Scott Bowron) courtesy New York Quilt Project, Museum of American Folk Art, New York City. (Collection of the Putnam County Historical Society, Cold Spring, New York) This quilt, made as a fundraiser for auction, contains one block stating that it was made by the "Ladies Aid Society of the North Highlands M.E. Church, organized 1898. Quilt pieced December 1904." Although some of the blocks (each of which is signed) have recognizable symbolism, others are highly personal designs, such as the one showing a moon and stars, with the notation "Full Moon April 29 5:40 A.M.," that give no clue to their importance to the makers. Several are amusing, such as the block with four smiling cats that says "Rough on Rats," or the one showing three cats with a verse "Tom, Dick, and Harry/ Vowed never to marry/ In the Good Old Summertime."

Indebted to the Ladies

"…we have been greatly indebted to the ladies of our congregation for material aid. By their sewing society &c. they have furnished fuel and lights and kept up repairs."[1]

"Olive Hill [Church] will have an ice cream supper June 16 [1884]. They will sell the wheel quilt at that time, the proceeds will be used to finish the church.…This same wheel quilt was a design of a wheel…for which names were solicited with 10 cents for placing the name on the tire, 25 cents on a spoke, and 50 cents on the hub. Much money was raised in this way, different ladies vieing [sic] with each other in securing the most names and money on their block."[2]

"One thousand dollars for the Red Cross can be raised on a memorial quilt.…A Quilt Campaign is especially adapted to church auxiliaries, women's clubs, and organized groups of women in small towns.…"[3]

For generations, women have made quilts for causes close to their hearts—from helping the needy to missionary societies, to church buildings, to abolition, to temperance, to war—but prior to the nineteenth century women had a minimum of free time to devote to such causes. Meeting the basic everyday needs of their families left little energy for responding to social issues or extensive humanitarian involvement, although local charitable actions were common as part of the community solidarity that was so crucial to the development of this country. By the early nineteenth century, however, one of the areas of women's work that claimed the most time—the provision of textiles and clothing for their families—began to lessen as factory-made cloth and prespun thread and yarn became available on a broad scale, thus paving the way for many women to begin to look outward. The religious revival that began about this time provided an avenue of focus and a means of expression of which women began to take full advantage.

Although women's participation as decisionmakers in the church was severely limited, the surge of growth in missionary societies of all denominations that accompanied the religious revival supplied women with opportunities to take on more active roles. The prevailing contemporary emphasis on "women's sphere" that already viewed women as keepers of home and hearth was expanded to include the guardianship of the moral and spiritual well-being of the family, and, by extension, the community. Because of the prevailing view of women as intrinsically more pious and morally superior,[4] it is not surprising that the majority of the active membership of many churches was composed of women, thus giving them, by sheer virtue of their numbers, an opportunity to influence the church establishment in a tangible way. Missionary, ladies'-aid, and auxiliary societies affiliated with the churches—societies often organized, managed, and maintained by women (although a law persisted in Massachusetts until 1840 that made it illegal for a woman to serve as treasurer of such societies unless a man assumed responsibility for her[5])—became major sources of revenue and, as such, of great importance to the churches. These groups provided funds for local church needs—from construction and upkeep of a church to paying the minister's salary—as well as for helping to spread the Gospel through missionary work and aiding the needy through various types of charitable work. Church maintenance has remained an underlying theme in fundraising efforts even until today, but after about 1830 interest in supporting various social reforms became at least as important—and sometimes superseded—raising funds to aid missionary work and the needy. That women viewed participation in such efforts as part of their social role was spelled out by one woman as she noted in her diary that "the time has come when I must do my part socially" as she prepared to join in the work of her church,[6] and the records of a church sewing society state that "the primary objective of our Society is to aid in deferring the expenses of the church. The second is to promote the social interests of its members and friends."[7]

A favorite means of raising revenue for the ambitious undertakings delineated by these societies was through sewing, a skill that lent itself admirably to the thousands—if not tens of thousands—of quilts made for fundraising purposes over the years. The societies also provided some of the few opportunities for house-tied women to gather together for a bit of social interchange and relaxation as they worked on their various projects, an opportunity to escape, however briefly, from the many demands and constraints of the nineteenth-century home in a manner that would be approved by both spouse and community.[8]

74. Farmer's Bowknot with Eastern Stars; members of Women's Relief Corps #126; possibly midwestern United States; 1891; pieced cotton; 80″ x 80″. (Photograph courtesy Laura Fisher/ Antique Quilts and Americana, New York City) The stars on this quilt may connect it with the Order of the Eastern Star, the women's branch of the Masons. The group was involved in many charitable endeavors, and this quilt was probably made as a fundraiser for one of them. It also serves to document the structure of the organization, as officers' names and titles are listed in the central star.

Although many of the gatherings offered at least token service to the religious umbrella under which they worked through uplifting lectures or Bible readings during the time they gathered to work, there was also often a lighter side to the gatherings, and diaries indicate that an equal amount of empathy, advice, patterns, recipes, and gossip were exchanged with every stitch of thread: "This afternoon I go to Sewing Society at Mr. Pierces. I suppose the affairs of the town will be discussed over the quilt."[9]

By the middle of the nineteenth century, ladies'-aid societies were contributing increasingly substantial portions of many church budgets through their fundraising efforts. The monies raised paid off debts, covered the minister's salary or education, paid for church repairs and maintenance, provided funds for new buildings, and met humanitarian needs as well. Money went to needy people in the community, to orphanages, church missionaries, hospitals, or homes for the aged and homeless, and, in this century, to external institutions such as the Red Cross. In spite of Elizabeth Cady Stanton's disdain for women's support of a ministry that did not even support their rights, fundraising was one way that women could gain some semblance of power within the male-dominated church hierarchy; they often had full control over the money that they raised, and it would well behoove a minister who depended on the efforts of the women of his congregation for his salary to pay some attention to their interests and needs.

There were several variations of the fundraising quilt, and one of the most popular—and long-lived—has been the signature fundraiser. Shortly after the middle of the nineteenth century the fad for putting names on quilts began to find a niche in the fundraising arena, and, by the latter part of the century, the fashion was well-developed.[10] These inscribed, signature, or autograph quilts (as they are variously called), which involved an exchange of money for including a name on a quilt, may be separated into two major categories, although it is not always easy to place a specific quilt within a category

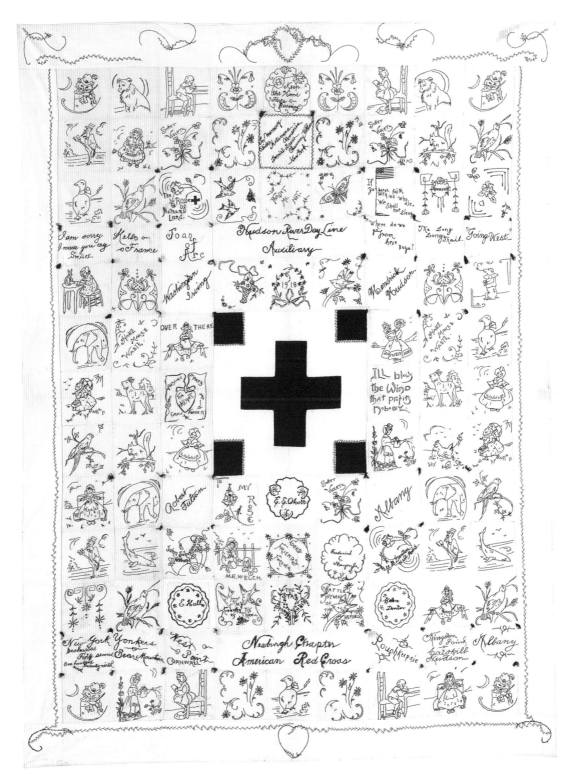

75. Red Cross Fundraiser; members of the Hudson River Dayliner Auxiliary of the Red Cross; Newburgh, New York; c. 1918; pieced, appliquéd, and embroidered cotton; 88″ x 66″. Photograph courtesy Laura Fisher/Antique Quilts and Americana, New York City. (Private collection) Many of the traditional and easily available penny-square blocks that form the basis of this fundraising quilt have been embellished with old adages ("Ill blows the wind that profits nobody," "Haste makes waste") or World War I slogans ("Over there," "The Rose of No Man's Land," "Keep the home fires burning"). Some blocks seem to have been made in memory of local soldiers; other show the names of the ships of the Dayline, a popular company that ran boats on the Hudson River from New York City north. The verse, "If ye break faith/ with us who die, / We shall not sleep," is from John McCrae's famous poem, "In Flanders Fields," first published in 1915.

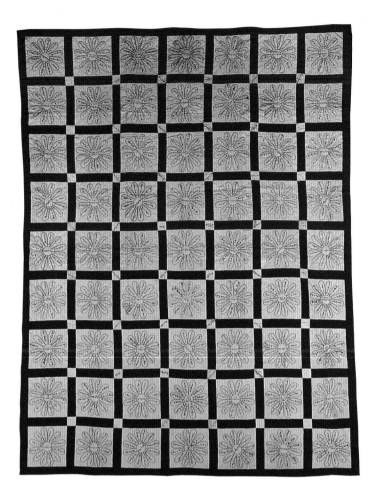

77. Detail—Fundraiser; present whereabouts unknown; third quarter of the nineteenth century; appliquéd cotton. This block, from a fundraiser quilt made for an unknown purpose, includes a notation of the individual amounts, ranging from ten cents to forty cents, donated by participants. It appears as if one person did all the inscriptions, given the evenness of the hand.

76. Embroidered Signatures; makers unknown; location unknown; c. 1905; pieced and embroidered cotton; size unavailable. (Collection of The Brooklyn Museum, Brooklyn, New York; Gift of Mrs. C.W. Palmer) This type of quilt was being made by church and school groups around the country as a part of fundraising efforts. With its capacity for including the names of a large number of contributors (nearly 900 are included here), the quilt had the potential for raising a significant amount of money for some worthy project.

78. Star; makers unknown; location unknown; 1928; appliquéd and embroidered cotton; 88½″ x 79″. Photograph by Scott Bowron. (Courtesy Susan Parrish Antiques, New York City) This quilt most likely served a double purpose—first as a subscription or tithing quilt and then as a presentation gift to the church pastor, whose name—Rev. A.C. Saxman—is embroidered in the center star, along with the date. The large number of names on the quilt, as well as the fact that both men and women are represented, point to it being one that raised money from the entire church membership; the names around the central star may have been more prominent members (or trustees) or those who contributed larger amounts. The quilt appears never to have been washed, as the pencil marks for the quilting are still visible in many places.

unless its history is well-known or unless a hint is given within the quilt itself. There is often not a great deal of difference in style, as both types frequently made lavish use of the names to supplement or actually create the quilt's pattern.

The first type, Subscription quilts, are so called because those involved in the fundraising effort would gather monetary subscriptions (or donations) from an individual or business who wished to have their name added to the quilt. The funds raised were often for some specific project, and contributors would each pay a small amount—sometimes only a few cents, sometimes as much as fifty cents or even one dollar per name—to have their names embroidered on a quilt. While Subscription quilts were a form used by many different community institutions, the second type, a tithing, or revenue, quilt was strictly church-related. It contained the names of church members who pledged specific sums of money to the church treasury, to be used either for specific projects or for ongoing church upkeep. The amounts pledged on tithing quilts were likely to vary more than those on Subscription quilts. There might be a minimum amount suggested by the church, but the general principle seemed to be to give in keeping with one's abilities or position; sometimes the amount of the donation was even embroidered along with the name.

With either type of quilt, the amount of money donated could determine the position of a name or how prominent a place it might be given. The pattern chosen for the quilt would also play a part, for a design such as Wagon Wheels or Double T did not allow for a great deal of leeway in size or position of a name, while an Album or a Star variation provided more opportunity for gradations of prominence. The number of names found on such quilts varied widely, from as few as fifty to well over one thousand. Although the amounts raised by some of these efforts might not seem worth much today—some quilts, even those with several hundred names on them, might have raised only two or three hundred dollars (Lasansky notes one with one thousand two hundred names that raised $337.00, at a cost of six to ten cents per name[11])—it must be remembered that, at a time when a simple frame church could be built for as little as $700, a fundraiser that could bring in a quarter to one-half of the amount needed was not to be ignored.[12] Some fundraising efforts had much more spectacular results, of course, and a quilt made in 1882 by church groups for the Kentucky Baptist Orphans Home is known to have raised over $5,000 alone.

Names on these quilts were embroidered more often than written in ink, and sometimes the names themselves formed the only pattern. In some examples, the quilt surface has been so covered with names that no discernible pattern can be seen, while in others the names have been placed to form an appealing visual image.

Many fundraisers were based on repetitive pattern blocks such as Setting Sun, Double T, and Wagon Wheels or Stars in their many variations. In these, the names were embroidered or inked in and around the spokes or points and, if the group had been particularly successful in its fundraising efforts, on the sashing and borders as well. More elaborate versions used Dresden Plate variations or, during the height of the fad for Crazy quilts, unique combinations that were restricted only by the imagination of the makers.

Prior to 1900, fundraising quilts were usually raffled once they were completed, raising even more money for their cause (and sometimes the raffles raised far more money than the original subscription effort). However, the end of the nineteenth century saw a growing conservatism in some sects, and "playing at games of chance" became an activity that could lead to expulsion from the mother group for a specific church.[13] Raffles were considered "games of chance," so this lucrative method of adding to church coffers disappeared in many areas. (Some churches managed to get around the letter of the law by offering a stick of gum or a piece of candy along with the raffle ticket; thus making the activity a "purchase" or "donation" rather than "gambling."[14]) Fundraising quilts continued to be made, however, and after the initial tithing or subscription efforts were complete, the quilts might then find their way into church auctions, which were considered acceptable activities as chance was not involved, or they would be used as presentation gifts to the minister or his wife or other prominent members of the community. Sometimes, when a quilt was auctioned, the purchaser would present it back to the church or the group that made it so that it could be auctioned again and raise still more money, or the buyer might present it to the person who had devoted the most energy to the fundraising effort.

Around the turn of the twentieth century a popular type of fundraising quilt was one that featured the signatures of famous people. For these, a piece of fabric would be sent to the person along with a letter explaining the cause for which the signature was requested. When the fabric was returned, signed in indelible ink, it was worked into the pattern of the quilt. Occasionally the makers of the quilt might embroider over the signatures, but often they were left plain. This trend may have been a belated spinoff of the earlier autograph album fad or a natural flow from the collecting of signed photographs or papers from popular personages of the day. Actors, actresses, singers, and dancers were probably considered a little too risqué for church groups, however, so the signatures garnered for these efforts tended to be political. Peto mentions a Blue Eagle quilt made by the Women's Missionary Society of the Methodist Episcopal Church of Calhoun, Kentucky, that features forty-eight stars, each bearing an embroi-

79. Crazy; ladies of the Old Dutch Reformed Church; Brooklyn, New York; c. 1885; pieced and embroidered mixed fabrics with bobbin lace; 62″ x 140″. (Collection of The Brooklyn Museum, Brooklyn, New York; Gift of Mrs. Arrietta Smith) The immense diversity that can be found in Crazy quilts is easily seen in this example, in which each square was made by a different church lady. The finished squares were sewn together and given a decorative edging, then raffled to raise money for the church. The quilt was owned by Matilda Wykcoff Rapelfe (b. 1849), who may well have also been one of the makers.

80. Crazy; The Ladies Aid Society, First Presbyterian Church; New York, New York; 1907–1908; appliquéd and embroidered satin, silk, and ribbon; 86¾″ x 105½″. (Collection of The Smithsonian Institution, Washington, D.C.; Gift of Emilie Noakes Manly in honor of Margaret Clarke Goodall Bradley) This very creative fundraising project contains 365 signatures, including those of President Theodore Roosevelt and members of his Cabinet (on the stripes of the American flag) and governors of forty-six states (on the rays surrounding "E Pluribus Unum"). Margaret Clarke Goodall Bradley, a member of the Society, played a major part in the work on this piece, and, although she did not win the raffle, the winner presented it to her in appreciation of her efforts.

81. Dresden Plate Variation; made by members of the Cardus Class of West Avenue United Methodist Church; Rochester, New York; 1915–1920; pieced and appliquéd silk and taffeta; 77" x 76". Photograph by Scott Bowron courtesy New York Quilt Project, Museum of American Folk Art, New York City. (Collection of the West Avenue United Methodist Church) Most of the more than 200 signatures on this quilt were members of the Cardus Sunday school class, and each student paid a small fee to place his or her name on the quilt in order to help raise money for their church. Class members probably contributed scraps of fabric as well in order to provide the extensive array that form the Dresden Plates.

82. Sampler Album; made by the Ladies of the Mt. Sinai Church Group; Miller Place, New York; 1846–1847; pieced and appliquéd cotton; 97″ x 99″. Photograph by Scott Bowron courtesy New York Quilt Project, Museum of American Folk Art, New York City. Each block in this quilt was made and signed by a member of the Mt. Sinai Congregational Church, which served three towns on the north shore of Long Island. Although the purpose for which it was made and the amount of money raised is now lost, the careful crafting of the blocks, each quilted separately, indicate that the contributors wished to do their best for this church project. The quilt is now known as "The Bird of Paradise" quilt because the center block contains the following poem: "Oh what of the land thou doest hover o'er,/ Bright bird of the tireless wing?/ Say is there no grief on that peaceful shore/ And blooms there eternal spring?/ From far away in my beautiful home,/ From all that to sin can entice,/ High o'er your earth and its sorrows I soar,/ I'm a bird of paradise." Though now faded and stained from age and use, the quilt retains a strong sense of its former glory. (Collection of Margaret D. Gass)

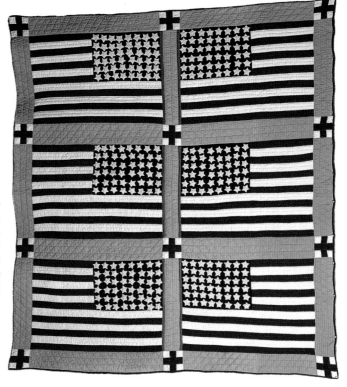

83. Flag; members of the Pleasant View Home Demonstration Club; Pleasant View, Oklahoma; 1942; pieced cotton; 86″ x 76″. Photograph by Blunck Studios. (Collection of Cindy's Quilts, Clinton, Oklahoma) This quilt, made as a fundraiser for a home-demonstration club during World War II, reflects the patriotism of the times. Home-demonstration clubs were popular in the rural areas of the Midwest and western United States and contributed to the war effort in many ways.

dered outline of a state and the signature of the governor of that state.[15] Cozart mentions a quilt made by a group of Presbyterian church women in Victoria, Illinois, that used a similar concept, but rather than signatures, the women collected scraps of fabric from famous people and made a Crazy quilt from them. The project took five years, but the finished product sold for nearly $1,000, which was the goal set by the group. Only the signatures of Ulysses S. Grant and Mrs. Grover Cleveland appear on the quilt; the fabrics were numbered and then listed in a book with the name of the contributer of each piece.[16]

The signature fundraisers served one purpose at the time of their creation, but today they have a different benefit for us. Those built on local signatures provide a reflection of a community, be it a family, church, school, organization, or town. By providing a sense of the extent of local families or the relationships between different families and communities, such quilts can offer tantalizing glimpses into the social structure and values of a time gone by. The quilts that made use of the names of the celebrities of the time give some insight into the political scene and even serve to remind us of those who once served the public interests of the day. *Godey's Lady's Book*, in a description of an 1864 quilt with 356 signatures, was not far off in noting that future generations would see it "not only as a marvel of women's ingenious and intellectual industry; but as affording an idea of the civilization of our times, and also giving a notion of the persons as estimed in history."[17]

Signature quilts were not the only type of quilts used as fundraisers. Some quilts were made specifically for raffle or auction, and Album or Sampler quilts were often favored for this effort, with the signatures of the makers of each block the only names appearing—if at all—on the quilt. Album quilts, especially if created by a church group, often included religious symbols such as crosses, harps, bibles, angels, and the anchor of hope. Repetitive blocks were often used, as women involved in the quiltmaking effort could work on the blocks at home and then gather to join and quilt once enough blocks were completed. For these quilts, patterns with a religious connotation, such as Crown of Thorns, Christian Cross, Job's Tears, or Jacob's Ladder, might be chosen if a church were the sponsor of the fundraising activity. The use of Crazy quilts as fundraisers coincided with the Crazy craze, although some continued to be made well into this century. Sometimes a quilt would include a representation of the church or school with which the makers were affiliated, and one enterprising group involved in raising funds for a new building even stitched a blueprint of the proposed church to their quilt.[18] The

additional historical benefit of such quilts is that a record is kept of what the earlier buildings may have looked like, as time, fire, expansion, or remodeling may have significantly changed the appearance today.

The ties between quilting and fundraising were firmly grounded by the end of the nineteenth century and have continued well into the twentieth century. Groups with many different affiliations—both religious and lay—have successfully used this tried-and-true method of raising money over the years, and the nostalgic lure of the quilt seems as potent a draw as ever. Churches, especially in rural areas, have remained the chief makers and users of fundraising quilts. In some parts of the country, the tradition is institutionalized; in the Mennonite Church, for example, local church groups make any number of quilts every year, some of which are kept for local use for families in need. Others are provided to the Church's Central Committee for distribution to worldwide relief projects, and one from each group (usually the "best" quilt) is sent to the Central Committee for its annual auction to raise funds for the ongoing work of the Church.[19] The quality of the quilts at these auctions is well known, and the annual auction will draw bidders from all over the country, resulting in a profitable fundraising effort for the Central Committee.

Today schools, libraries, senior-citizen groups, and many others active on local levels regularly include quilts made communally by their members as annual raffle prizes or as part of fundraising auctions. Proceeds may go for self-serving ends, such as high-school trips, or be used to help communities in many ways—from housing the homeless and feeding the hungry, to restoring historic buildings, to buying books for a library, or to a variety of other charitable purposes. Unlike the church groups, which have a long-term character that encourages intimacy and sharing among the members, many of the groups today are short-term, created for a specific purpose, such as restoring an old school building, and dissolved when the stated goal has been attained. Sometimes, however, those involved have rediscovered the simple pleasures to be found in shared work and mutual support and have continued the group long past the realization of the original objective. Although new targets and tasks may be set to give a structure to the group, the quilting is perhaps the excuse, and the sharing the real reason for participating. One woman, in explaining her reason for continuing her attendance at a church quilting group, noted that the real reason she went was for "the camaraderie and to get to know my neighbors better. [Sometimes] they'd laugh so much they couldn't even sew."[20]

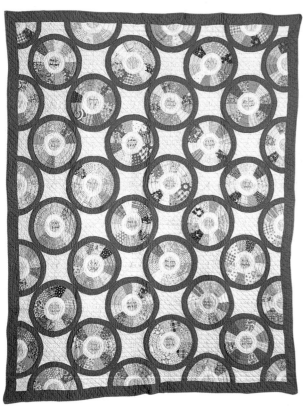

84. Dresden Plate Variation; unknown makers; Washington, D.C.; 1930s; pieced cotton; 82″ x 64″. Photograph by Scott Bowron. (Courtesy Judith and James Milne, Inc., New York City) Each plate in this bright quilt carries an embroidered name at its center. It was likely made by a high school class either as a token of friendship for a teacher or as a class fundraiser. The quilt was probably assembled by one person, with the white and blue fabric purchased for this purpose, but the wide variety of fabrics included in the "plates" point to the possibility of several makers for them, as does the variation in the skill shown in the embroidery of the names.

85. Schoolhouse; Aurelie Stack and members and friends of the North Fork Quilters; Mattituck, New York; 1989; pieced and appliquéd cotton; 96″ x 72″. Photograph by Daniel Jones courtesy Aurelie Stack. This quilt was made by a group of women who had a clear goal in mind. It was raffled to help defray the cost of relocating the Old Bay View Schoolhouse, which was built in 1822 and was one of the earliest one-room district schools in New York State, from its original location to the grounds of the Southold Historical Society in Mattituck, New York. Each of the fourteen Schoolhouse blocks was made by a different woman, and Aurelie Stack, who masterminded the project, made the center panel and pieced the quilt. The names of all those who worked on the quilt are embroidered on the back; their efforts raised nearly $10,000 for the project. The forty-eight-star flag above the schoolhouse is a cigar flannel (1900–1920); it was chosen because that was the flag in use when the school closed its doors in 1925 after 103 years.

86, 87. A group of women at work on a popular 1930s design (fig. 86) and the finished quilt being proudly displayed (fig. 87). (Collections of Library of Congress, Washington, D.C.)

88. Shoo Fly; made by Connecticut WCTU members; c. 1887; pieced silks and taffetas, with embroidery and ink work; 73″ x 72½″. Photograph by Scott Bowron. (Collection of National Woman's Christian Temperance Union, Evanston, Illinois) This quilt, said to have been presented to Frances Willard, the WCTU's leading force for many years, served as a sort of state roster for the Connecticut chapter of the organization, with names of state leaders and local chapters written or stitched on the quilt. The WCTU initials, embroidered in the official colors of the organization, appear in the four corners of the inner square. The women who worked this piece used their obvious sewing skills to make a bold and elegant statement of their commitment to their beliefs.

Pricking the Social Conscience

"May the points of our needles prick the slave owner's conscience."
—Sarah Grimké

"The day will come when, beside the death-sentence of a woman who was burned as a witch…beside the block from which a woman was sold as a slave…and beside the liquor license that was issued by the State of Illinois to ruin its young men, there will hang this beautiful quilt to which young men and women will point with pride and say, 'There is the name of my great-grandmother, who took part in Ohio's great crusade.'"
—Frances E. Willard, WCTU National Convention, 1877

"Peace binds the pieces….Peace is the backing of our patchwork quilt."[1]

Sewing, benevolence, social reform, and fundraising have long been closely entwined in women's lives, and it is often difficult to determine where one stops and another starts. It is but a short step from making quilts for the needy, for church needs, or for missionaries to making quilts for a social or political cause, to let the needle say what society might otherwise condemn, and to raise money by doing so. As the nineteenth century progressed, women used their needlework more and more to draw attention to problems in which they were interested and thereby found a way to give voice to their concerns and beliefs at a time when they often had little or no direct control over the issues of the day. Their needlework often carried messages, evangelistic or otherwise, to emphasize their points of view quietly. Sewing to raise money provided an ideal means to participate in social reform movements and draw public attention to issues and concerns—a means that still works today.

A woman might also find the needed companionship of like-minded peers in one of the many benevolent organizations that grew up in the nineteenth century as she grappled with some of the increasingly urgent issues of the day.[2] The format of these church-related benevolent societies lent itself well to new interests as women began to recognize the power of unity and to make fuller use of the organizational skills they had gained in these groups. Sometimes spurred by their ministers—"Your voice should be heard the loudest and the first in defense of that domestic peace which it is your peculiar province to secure….God and the perishing hopes of the world demand that you direct your influence against every system which dares to invade the repose of the family circle"[3]—they established societies for the abolition of slavery and alcohol and for promotion of equal rights for women, alongside those whose mission remained concerned with the alleviation of the lot of the poor and the heathen. In 1861, however, social and moral issues were set aside as the Civil War took precedence over all other concerns and women committed their needles to meet their soldiers' needs.

The massive war-relief effort served to hone women's organizational skills even further and gave them some better understanding of the impact that they could have when working together. Many women emerged from the war years with a greater determination to become active participants in social reform rather than passive observers and turned their energies—and their needles—even more strongly to those ills of society that concerned them the most. Perhaps chief among those concerns was the abuse of alcohol, which had contributed to the deterioration and abuse of so many families. In the early part of the nineteenth century, almost three times as much alcohol was consumed per capita as is done today. Ale, or even whiskey, was consumed at all meals, some wages were paid in whiskey or rum, and saloons were the favorite meeting places for men. In the frontier heydays, Cheyenne, Wyoming, for example, could boast one saloon per one hundred drinkers, while the 1870s in Ohio saw an astounding ratio of one to thirty in the more populated areas.[4]

Male-organized, clergymen-dominated temperance societies had been around since the 1820s, but by the mid-1850s they had lost their momentum as many of the leaders were also active abolitionists, and it is probable that this cause supplanted temperance in its need and immediacy. It was not until after the Civil War, when women became full (if often separate) participants rather than silent partners, that the movement became truly effective.[5] Inspiration for revival came from Dr. Dioclesian Lewis, who called for women to go into saloons and pray with saloon keepers and bartenders. The time was ripe for such action; the temperance movement had failed

89. Hexagon Signature; Woman's Christian Temperance Union members; Schenectady, New York; 1904; pieced cotton; 77″ x 52½″. (Collection of New York State Museum, Albany, New York) Every block contains a quote from the New Testament that reinforces the goals of the Woman's Christian Temperance Union, which retained its influence well into this century: "Repent ye for the Kingdom of Heaven is at hand"; "As the Father hath loved me, so have I lovest you"; "Behold the Lamb of God, which taketh away the sins of the world"; "As many as I love I rebuke and chasten: be zealous therefore, and repent"; "Christ in you the hope of glory. Resist the devil and he will flee from you." The quilt may have been made as a fundraiser for the local WCTU chapter, but it would have served equally well as a banner.

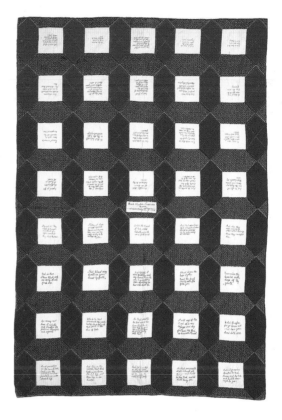

90. Crusade Quilt (back); made by Ohio WCTU members; 1876; pieced silks with ink and stamp work; 88½″ x 98″. Photograph courtesy of Hearts and Hands Media Arts, San Francisco. (Collection of National Woman's Christian Temperance Union, Evanston, Illinois) The signatures of three thousand women give vivid testimony to their beliefs on this quilt made in honor of Eliza Jane Trimble Thompson (better known as "Mother" Thompson) to commemorate the 1873 Women's Temperance Crusade in Ohio. The quilt was presented to her by Frances E. Willard at the National WCTU convention in 1877. The front of the quilt, as described in Willard's autobiography, "contained a square of a different color for each state represented, and had, in embroidery, upon each square the device and motto of the several auxiliary organizations. It was a beautiful example of woman's skill and taste in needle handicraft." (Frances E. Willard, *Glimpses of Fifty Years* [Chicago: H.J. Smith & Co., 1889], p. 77)

91. Suffragette quilt; makers unknown; Tuscarawas County, Ohio; c. 1912; pieced and embroidered cotton; 74″ x 72″. (Courtesy Susan Parrish Antiques, New York City) The Suffragettes promoted, publicized, and raised money for their goals in many ways, and one of the ways was through quilts that served both as political statements and as fundraisers. This wonderfully patriotic example could not help but draw attention to the cause, and it contains the signatures of over 350 Suffragettes, including that of Susan B. Anthony, leader of the organization.

miserably under male leadership, and women had proved their ability to work together effectively on a large scale in the organization of support for the Sanitary Commission during the Civil War. This was just the kind of cause at which they could succeed. Dr. Lewis's exhortations found fertile soil in Ohio, and women rallied to the cause. The Ohio Women's Temperance Crusade of 1873, led by "Mother" Eliza Thompson, was so successful that it resulted in the formal foundation of the Woman's Christian Temperance Union in 1874.

The WCTU, like all social-reform organizations, needed funds to support its work, and women turned to a method that had worked well for them in the past—the fundraising quilt. The first major WCTU fundraising quilt was started in 1875, in honor of Mother Thompson, for which "each local Union was requested to send…a square of silk of given dimensions, patchwork, quilted, or embroidered, but lined with linen, the usual gray color, and on that linen lining the names of all members who would send a dime or more must be written legibly, and if possible, in fadeless ink."[6] Over 3,000 women put their names on the quilt, and it paved the way for the making of many other quilts that continued to bring funds to the organization even into this century.[7]

Women also began to look beyond their prescribed place in society in the area of women's rights by the mid-nineteenth century. Discontent with existing discriminatory laws and customs became overt first with the convening of the 1848 Seneca Falls convention to discuss "the social, civil and religious condition and rights of women" and then with the 1852 Woman's Rights convention held in Syracuse, New York. It was there that Susan B. Anthony began her five-decade leadership of the movement, and it was Anthony who often found it effective to take her message to women as they gathered together to quilt.[8] As the Suffrage Movement gradually gained adherents and power in the latter part of the century, its supporters often found recourse to their needles to raise money and, in so doing, they also created dramatic testimonials that promoted their cause as well, as exemplified by one eye-catching flag-like quilt that carries Anthony's name along with at least 350 others. In working on projects such as this, women reinforced their own beliefs while finding a way to give public voice to the cause at hand.

Another example of women's commitment to a cause is seen in a social/political movement that began during the Great Depression. A Dr. Francis C. Townsend hatched a plan that would require the federal government to give each American over the age of sixty a pension of $200 a month (by comparison, a standard wage of $50.00 to $100.00 a month was considered a good income at this time), provided that they would spend the stipend in that month and thus pump money into the depressed economy. Totally unrealistic as the plan was from several points of view, it gained a great deal of popularity among many people (especially those of the senior age group), and Townsend clubs were started in many parts of the country. These groups often drew on the talented fingers

92. Suffragettes of all ages on the march. (Collections of Library of Congress, Washington, D.C.)

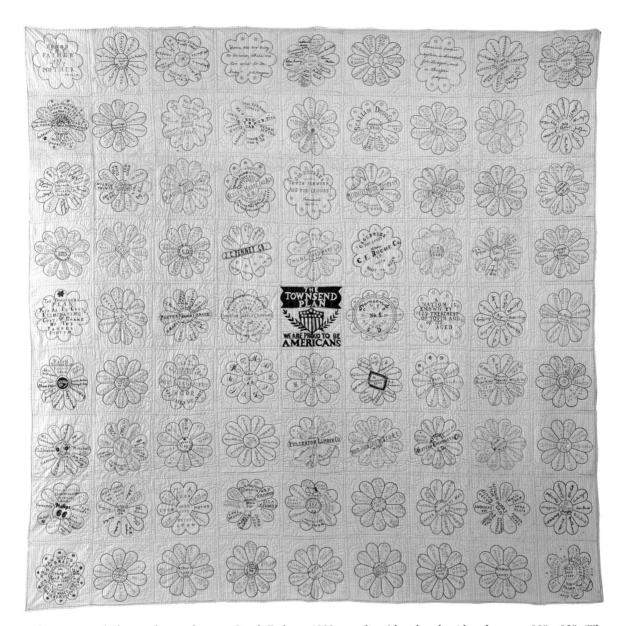

93. The Townsend Plan; makers unknown; South Dakota; 1930s; appliquéd and embroidered cotton; 96″ x 92″. (The Mitchell Wolfson, Jr. Collection, courtesy The Wolfsonian Foundation, Miami Beach, Florida, and Genoa, Italy) "No man without an honorable job at living wages under the Townsend Recovery Plan" and "A nation is known by its treatment of youth and of its aged" are some of the inscriptions on this unusual quilt. Another block, with the inscription "Youth for work, age for leisure," expresses the idea at the heart of The Townsend Plan. Made as a fundraiser, the quilt also makes a strong statement about the makers' commitment to this utopian scheme of economics that was popular during the Great Depression. Many of the blocks contain the names of local companies, some of which include the names of their employees.

of their members to create quilts that could be used to raise money to promote the Townsend "pie in the sky" and to bring pressure on the government to adopt the plan. The clubs raised revenue by charging for the privilege of having one's name embroidered on the quilt, and local businesses as well as individuals are often found to be contributors. Townsend himself made an unsuccessful attempt to gain the presidency in 1936; his plan continued to meet federal resistance and eventually died from lack of support (although it may have been one of the factors that eventually resulted in the Social Security Act), but a lively heritage was left behind in the form of quilts like the one illustrated in figure 93.

The period from the Great Depression through the Korean War was a time of lessened interest in quilting in general, and few quilts were made other than those created for utilitarian use. Women quilting together to support specific social or political causes was at a low ebb, although fundraiser quilts were still being made on a small scale and mostly in the more rural areas. The 1960s saw the birth of a new women's movement and a revitalization of the possibilities inherent in the individual and collective power of women as well as a resurgence of interest in crafts; in response to this latter trend, and spurred by the then upcoming Bicentennial Celebration, many women turned to quilting as a means of expressing their connection with those who had gone before and with defining their roots. As women came together to express their solidarity as women and as citizens with a common voice, they found, as had many before them, that quilting also provided an outlet for expression of many of their concerns, a means of confronting situations that seemed threatening to home and family, and a way of handling some of the frustrations of modern life by sharing concerns and finding strength in the understanding that often comes with such sharing. One of the earliest of these

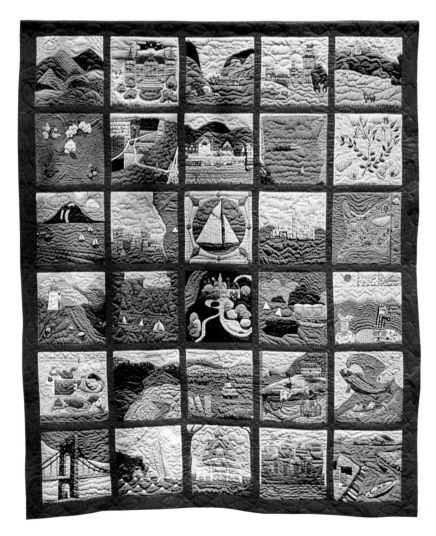

94. The Hudson River Quilt; Irene Preston and twenty-nine quilters; Croton-on-Hudson, New York; 1969–1972; pieced and appliquéd cotton; 96″ x 79″. Photograph courtesy Irene Miller. (Collection of Museum of American Folk Art, New York City; Gift of the J.M. Kaplan Fund) The quilt revival of the late 1960s and early 1970s had its roots in a "back to the land" movement that meshed in many ways with the nascent women's movement. As women came together at this time to realize the power inherent in shared beliefs and action, their voices were raised on behalf of many issues, and the environment figured prominently. This quilt was conceived by Irene Miller, who asked some friends to join her in raising money for the protection of the Hudson River through making a quilt. Each woman made a block representing some facet of life along the Hudson; they then joined and quilted the pieces in an old-fashioned quilting bee. After its completion, the quilt was sent on an eighteen-year round of exhibitions to raise awareness about the need to protect the river. When the quilt was finally auctioned in 1990, it raised $23,000 that was divided among three environmental groups dedicated to the well-being of the Hudson River. The quilt, considered "the first group quilt for a cause" of this era, has served as a model and inspiration for many others. (Quote from Bonnie Lehman, *Quilter's Newsletter Magazine*, June 1990, p. 89)

95. Soviet American Peace Quilt; Boise Peace Quilt Project, Soviet Women's Committee, and Mothers for Peace; 1985; pieced, appliquéd, and embroidered cottons. Photograph courtesy Boise Peace Quilt Project, Boise, Idaho. A cooperative product of Soviet and American women, this quilt, based on a friendship album format, is symbolic of the original goals of the Boise Peace Quilt Project—to build ties of friendship and understanding in the world, and to open lines of communication between people of all countries. The Boise Project, which started with a handful of people in 1981, has now involved hundreds of people around the world who, despite different social, cultural, and political beliefs, are committed to the concept of a safer and better world and use their quilts to help make their beliefs known. In the words of Pete Seeger, a strong supporter of the Project, "We'll stitch this world together yet!"

96. The Rosa Parks Quilt; Boise Peace Quilt Project; Boise, Idaho; 1992; pieced and appliquéd cottons, cotton blends; photo transfer, embroidery; 89″ x 100″. © Boise Peace Quilt Project. Photograph courtesy Boise Peace Quilt Project. With the lessening of tensions as the Cold War ebbs, the Boise Peace Quilt Project has turned its attention to other concerns. A recent quilt created by its members serves as a commemoration of Rosa Parks, a leading symbol of the Civil Rights movement in its early days, and a reminder to everyone that there is still much work to be done in the arena of civil and human rights both in the United States and around the world. The quilt contains many rose prints as a tribute to Ms. Parks's name.

projects that gave women a new voice was the Hudson River Quilt, conceived and organized by Irene Preston Miller beginning in 1969. Not only did the project succeed far beyond the makers' hopes in its fundraising goals, it brought invaluable attention on a national scale to the environmental issues that it wished to address.

The Hudson River Quilt was only the first of many quilts that have been made over the succeeding years to make a statement, to shed light on the ills and injustices of society, to garner public support for a worthy cause, and to help people cope with problems that are of a scale beyond what the individual or family can hope to deal with, yet which leave a sense of frustration or fear in their wake. Several quilt projects have been devoted to peace and disarmament, among which the best known are the Boise Peace Project, Quilters: Piece for Peace, and the Peace Ribbon, all of which have involved hundreds of people here and abroad. Although first and foremost intended as visual spurs to public consciousness of an issue, the quilts made by these groups have also very effectively helped to raise money that is used to further the cause. With the decrease in tensions as a result of the collapse of the former Soviet Union and a move toward a new world order, the Boise Peace Project has turned its energies to highlight other global issues, some of which deal with the environment and human rights. A quilt now on the frame acknowledges Lester Brown and the environmental impact work that the Worldwatch Institute, which he established, is carrying out; another quilt commemorates Rosa Parks, a pioneer in the civil rights struggle in the United States. The efforts of this very committed group keep these concerns constantly in the public eye and thus serve as a continuing visible prick to our consciences.

While many societal ills and concerns from homelessness to drunk driving to aging have been addressed through quilts made to highlight specific problems, in some cases literally tens of thousands of quilts are made as part of a practical solution to a problem and not only to raise the public's awareness. Just as women donated time, energy, and fabric to make quilts for the needy or for soldiers in the Civil War and World War I, so today women are working together to provide quilts as a concrete symbol of caring for children confined to hospitals and hospices. ABC Quilts, started in 1988 by Ellen Alhgren of Northwood, New Hampshire, as a response to the plight of babies and young children suffering from AIDS who are confined to hospitals, has contributed untold numbers of quilts to hospitals throughout the country in the five years since this voluntary effort began.[9] Quilts are made not only by adult groups but also by classes of school children and Scout groups.

Some regional coordinators for ABC Quilts, such as Donna Boyle in New York City, have found that the quilts are an ideal educational mechanism as well; Boyle says that when she visits schools to talk to children about making quilts for the project she may find herself giving an impromptu lecture on AIDS. She recalls her shock when one group of junior high students told her that "only drug pushers and gays get AIDS, not babies." Once these children were given a better understanding of the problem, they enthusiastically began a quilting project in their class because they wanted to help. ABC quilts are given to hospitals for distribution to AIDS babies and to other children in crisis conditions; Boyle notes that, for some, the quilt may be the only thing that the child can call its own, and all too frequently it may serve also as a shroud.

As with the ABC Quilts, many guilds and church groups have helped to supply quilts to Ronald McDonald houses, homes away from home that allow parents and siblings to be near terminally ill children in hospitals. The Ronald McDonald houses often provide quilts to the siblings as well as to the ill children so that these children may have some tangible bit of comfort of their own during a stressful family period. Many of the same groups making quilts for these two causes have extended their commitment to making quilts for chronically hospitalized adults as well.

The outpouring of help that has come about in response to such projects as these and many, many others has made it clear that commitment to a cause is still alive and well among the women of America. It is also clear that women—and men and children as well—are willing to put effort into a traditional and homely art that produces a visible token of concern; one that is often a small step toward alleviating the horror of the problem as well as providing a daily reminder that those who are suffering are not forgotten—that many people care. "Communal" takes on a whole new meaning when these visible symbols of deep commitment and personal involvement from thousands of people become part and parcel of everyday life. Yet the bottom line remains the same, whether the group consists of two or three women working on a quilt for a family in need or hundreds working individually or in small groups to contribute their poignant reminder to the NAMES Project AIDS Memorial Quilt (see Epilogue, pages 121–129) the belief in and commitment to a common cause and the desire to contribute to its solution in some small way, however humble.

97. Freehand Blocks; three-year-olds enrolled in Parkside Children's Workshop; Brooklyn, New York; 1991; pieced and painted cotton, muslin, flannel. Photograph by Karen Bell. (Courtesy ABC Quilts, Brooklyn, New York) These youngsters, with the help of their mothers (who did the sashing, backing, and tieing), made these lively drawings to help cheer up children less fortunate than themselves.

98. Stenciled Blocks; A.A.M. Club, Alfred Parrish Church; Alfred, Maine; 1992; pieced and stenciled cotton, cotton blends; 38¾" x 37¾". Photograph by Karen Bell. (Courtesy ABC Quilts, Brooklyn, New York) This is one of the thousands of crib quilts made by groups throughout the U.S.A. for the ABC Quilts project.

99. Fan Variation; various makers; Hokkaido, Japan; 1992; pieced and appliquéd cotton; 59" x 59". Photograph by Karen Bell. (Courtesy ABC Quilts, Brooklyn, New York) The Japanese characters on this quilt say it best—"Quilting is Communication." It was made by a group of women in Japan who had heard about the ABC Quilts project and wanted to show their support for it.

100. Detail—Patriotic; Cornelia Dow and others; Portland, Maine; 1864; pieced and appliquéd cotton with inscriptions and embroidery; 81″ x 71″. Photograph courtesy Hearts and Hands Media Arts, San Francisco. (Private collection) The central shield presents a visually dramatic statement of the strong pro-Union loyalties of the makers of this quilt.

Three Cheers for the Red, White, and Blue

"For the gay and happy soldier
We're contented as a dove,
But the man who will not enlist
Never can gain our love."

"If the rebels attack you, do run with the quilt
And safe to some fortress convey it;
For o'er the gaunt body of some old sesesh
We did not intend to display it."[1]

"I have never studied the art of paying compliments to women, but I must
say that if all that has been said by orators and poets since the creation of
the world in praise of women was applied to the women of America, it
would not do them justice for their conduct during this war."[2]

In spite of societal mores that have often placed limits on "appropriate" modes of expression for women, women have always managed to find ways of making their feelings and beliefs known, especially when patriotism is an issue. Patriotic expression has flourished in quiltmaking for many years, and there are untold numbers of quilts that include representations of Liberty bells, shields, stars and stripes, flags, eagles, and similar symbols, as well as the ubiquitous red, white, and blue—all visually dramatic, if otherwise silent, statements of the makers' beliefs and loyalties. As noted earlier, Freedom quilts for boys frequently contained one or more patriotic blocks, unspoken reminders to the recipients of where their duty lay besides giving the makers opportunities to express their own allegiance.

Patriotic expression in quilts has, perhaps, nowhere been more evident through the years than in times of war, when the need to express a loyal support for one's country is strong. This need burst into full flower during the Civil War, and it had a significant national impact on quilt-making and women's response. The War with Mexico in 1846, while arousing patriotic sentiment, had resulted in quilts made primarily to commemorate victories or to memorialize specific war heroes, but the Civil War saw women joining together to form an army of their own, with needles and thread as their weapons, as they moved to support their respective alliances, be it the Union or the Confederacy. As one contemporary source put it: "The women of the land could not follow those they loved in battle but...[they] had enlisted for the war, and there was nothing intermittent or spasmodic about their labor. As

long as the need lasted they were ready for service."[3] The need on both sides for clothing and bedding was great, and women responded enthusiastically. The benevolent societies that had been created to provide for the needy found it easy to turn their energies toward patriotism and to reform themselves almost overnight into soldiers'-aid societies. Those in the Union quickly became part of a widespread auxiliary network supporting the work of the United States Sanitary Commission, an organization formed in 1861 to supply the clothing, bedding, and nursing needs of the Union Army.

The Sanitary Commission saw thousands of Yankee women joined together not only to make many of the needed supplies but also to raise money through massive "Sanitary Fairs" for additional bandages and blankets, as well as medicine, food, and nurses.[4] By the end of the war, it is estimated that women's efforts on behalf of the Sanitary Commission had raised at least $25,000,000 for supplies and had provided at least 250,000 quilts and comforters for Union soldiers.[5] Frederick Law Olmstead, director of the Commission, noted, "Never, probably, was so large an army as well-supplied at a similar period of a great war." The work done by women during the war years has been likened to a "great national quilting party," with:

...the States so many patches, each of its own color or stuff, the boundaries of the nation the frame of the work; and at it [women] have gone, with needles and busy fingers, and their very heartstrings for thread...adding square to square, row to row;

101. Sampler Friendship; George Alfred Sutton, Margaret E. Dodge, and others; New York, New York; 1866–1902; pieced and appliquéd cotton with embroidery; 83⅛ x 75⅝″. (Collection of DAR Museum, Washington, D.C.; Given in memory of Nellie T. Sutton and George Alfred Sutton) Possibly inspired by the patriotic shield block given to him by his grandmother, Margaret E. Dodge, thirteen-year-old George Alfred Sutton collected the majority of the sampler blocks for this quilt in 1867 and 1868 from other relatives and friends. Many of the blocks are initialed or signed (one is embroidered "Phele Wing In My 88 Yr 1866"). Margaret Dodge later put together all the blocks that George had gathered, alternating them with simple blocks containing single circular patches, then had the piece quilted in 1902 at a quilting bee attended by several older ladies. The signed blocks provide a sampler of some of the most popular patterns used in Signature quilts (Chimney Sweep, Basket, Cracker on a Nine Patch, Eight-Pointed Star) as well as some blocks that are unique, if homely, designs.

102. Patriotic; makers unknown; Florence, Massachusetts; 1865; pieced and inscribed cotton; 53″ x 85″. Photograph courtesy America Hurrah Antiques, New York City. (Private collection) "Rally round the flag boys!" and the Stars and Stripes make it clear that this quilt was destined for a Union soldier. Although it is the right size for an army cot, the fine condition of the piece makes it unlikely that it was ever used. The inscriptions carry a range of messages intended to strengthen a soldier's will, from the militaristic ("REBELS: They mock our peaceful labor/ They scorn our useful toil/ But on their vain pretensions/ The blow will surely fall!") to the moralistic ("Touch not intoxicating drinks" and "Touch not tobacco—a curse on it"). The variation in handwriting and the fact that each block was individually quilted underlines the communality of this effort.

103. Wheel of Mystery (sometimes called Winding Ways); members of the Boston Street Aid Society; Lynn, Massachusetts; c. 1886; pieced cotton; 88″ x 88″. Photograph courtesy of Laura Fisher/ Antique Quilts and Americana, New York City. (Lynn Historical Society, Lynn, Massachusetts) A wealth of historical information about the Boston Street Aid Society from 1851 to 1886 is included in the inked inscriptions on this quilt. Not only are rolls of officers and members noted, but also projects important to the Society, along with transcriptions of thank-you letters received from the recipients of the Society's largesse, including the U.S. Sanitary Commission. Tidbits of the early history of the group include a note that the Society's twenty-seven founders in 1851 assessed themselves $1.50 per year and also agreed to bind shoes to raise money to furnish a church to be built on Boston Street. Although the quilt was probably originally made as a fundraiser for the Society, its role in the historical documentation of the group is now invaluable.

allowing no piece to escape their plan of Union; until the territorial area of the loyal states is all of a piece, first tacked and basted, then sewed and stitched by women's hands, wet often with women's tears, and woven in with women's prayers; and now at length you might truly say the National Quilt—all striped and starred—will tear anywhere sooner than in the seams, which they have joined in a blessed and inseparable unity![6]

The scope of effort on behalf of the Sanitary Commission is captured in part on a quilt made in the 1880s by members of the Boston Street Aid Society, who were clearly proud of the part their predecessors had played during the war. They transcribed on the blocks of this quilt letters of thanks received from the Sanitary Commission as well as records of the goods contributed by the Society, providing a concrete history of one group's involvement:

Please express the thanks of Sanitary Commission to the Ladies of Boston St. Aid Society for their kindly and valuable contribution. The articles will be forwarded immediately and will doubtless prove highly acceptable and useful to our brave soldiers.

I have the pleasure to acknowledge the rec. of a welcome box of supplies from the B. St. Aid Soc. of Lynn. The box shall be sent on its way to…Richmond to give its share of aid and comfort to those who stand so sorely in need.

Sent to the Sanitary Commission 1861:
Comforters 32. Pillows 23. Sheets 22. Pillow Cases 23. Large bale of old Pillow Cases, Sheets. Large bundles of old linen shirts, flannel shirts 19, bleached shirts 10, flannel drawers 19, 3 dressing gowns, large bundle hand "k"s, 3 blankets, 6 prs slippers, towels, napkins, woolen shawls, bandages, tin [?] balls, quilt cushions, large lot of stationery, medicines, cordials…in large quantities, All of which are dearly acknowledged by the officers of the U.S. Sanitary Commission.

The war inspired many women to enhance their quilts with patriotic motifs. Some groups inscribed their quilts, meant for soldiers at the front, with their names and stirring patriotic sentiments to lend encouragement as well as to underline the love and support of those who waited at home. A stunning example of the fervid patriotism that women felt but often were restricted from expressing publicly by the mores of the times is seen in a quilt created by a group in Maine, who combined symbols and sayings to articulate their passionate commitment to the Union cause. Many of the inscriptions on the quilt are blatant—sometimes even bloodthirsty—statements of partisanship and plays on words that leave the reader in

no doubt of the makers' sentiments and loyalties: "The leaves that least become a warrior's brow are leaves of absence"; "While our fingers guide the needle, Our thoughts are intense (in tents)"; When you find the white men, Union-hating white men, Let your cannon play! Where you find the black men, True and loyal black men, Let 'em run away! Break off their chains boys! Strick [sic] off their chains boys! And let 'em run away!" "[And so] sail on, O Ship of State! Sail on, O Union strong and great! Humanity with all its fears, With all its hopes of future years, Is hanging breathless on thy fate!" Flag quilts, another method of expressing patriotism, also gained great popularity, both to send to soldiers and for private use. Caroline Richards' sewing group in Canandaigua, New York, enthusiastically adopted this fad, as described in her diary:

May 1861—The girls in our society say that if any of the members do send a soldier to the war, they shall have a flag bed quilt, made by the society, and have the girls' names on the stars.

May 1863—We were talking about how many of us girls would be entitled to flag bed quilts, and, according to the rules, they said that, up to date, Abbie Clark and I were the only ones.

July 15, 1866—The girls of the Society have sent me my flag bed quilt, which they have just finished.…It is done beautifully. Bessie Seymour wrote the names on the stars. In the center they used six stars for "Three rousing cheers for the Union."[7]

Although the Confederacy had no agency comparable to the Sanitary Commission, the women of the South were no less diligent in trying to meet the needs of their "boys in gray."[8] Early on, sewing societies were formed to provide uniforms, socks, and bedding for the Confederate Army, and the lovely and delicate coverlet designs of happier times quickly gave way to more practical quilts. As the war dragged on and materials became more and more scarce (while rich in cotton, the raw material of many textiles, the South had few manufacturing resources), many groups turned to the technology of earlier years. Spinning wheels and looms once more became household items; spinning bees replaced quilting bees as homespun became the order of the day.[9] Mary High Prince, a staunch supporter of the Confederacy, was one of the makers and signers of a fundraiser Basket quilt made during the war, one of many quilts that were created by individuals and local groups to raise money to supply the Confederacy with the necessities of war. Many years later, in 1910, she eloquently captured the pride and the difficulties of the war in an inscription she embroidered on a commemorative pillow made from scraps of homespun from dresses worn by her and her friends:

104. Patriotic; Cornelia Dow and others; Portland, Maine; 1864; pieced and appliquéd cotton with inscriptions and embroidery; 81″ x 71″. Photograph courtesy Kentucky Historical Society, Frankfort, Kentucky. (Private collection) The many sayings inscribed here leave no doubt as to the Union sympathies of the makers of this quilt. Cornelia Dow, wife of a brigadier general in the Union Army who had been released from a Confederate prison as an exchange prisoner about the time the quilt was made, was probably one of the main instigators in its creation. The sentiments expressed range from blatantly militaristic to satirical and amusing, and many of the blocks are embellished with drawings or stamps of flags and other patriotic motifs.

105, 106. Star blocks from the Dow Patriotic quilt (fig. 104), showing some of the many stirring verses and statements that embellish this quilt. Photograph courtesy Hearts and Hands Media Arts, San Francisco. (Private collection)

107. Flag; members of the Young Ladies Sewing Society; Canandaigua, New York; c. 1866; pieced cotton; 81″ x 70½″. (Collection of Ontario County Historical Society, Canandaigua, New York; Gift of Mr. Clark Williams) The girls who comprised the Young Ladies Sewing Society had pledged to make a flag quilt for each of their members whose fiancé went to war in order to honor the service that their menfolk were providing the Union cause. This one was made for Abbie (or Abby) Clark, who was engaged to George N. Williams. The thirty-five stars contain the names of twenty-eight of those who worked on it, including that of Caroline Cowles Richards (signed here as "Carrie C. Richards), whose diary has made the efforts of this group well-known. The central star carries the saying "Three Rousing Cheers for the Union"; on several other stars are inked patriotic or marriage-related sayings: "He helped his country/ in her need/ And fought/ right loyally"; "Enfold them in the/ Stars and Stripes"; "Remember 'tis *For life*"; "Sweet be thy dreams."

"July 15, 1866: It kept the girls busy to get Abby Clark's quilt and mine finished within one month. They hope the rest of the girls will postpone their nuptials till there is a change in the weather. Mercury stands 90 degrees in the shade."
—Caroline Cowles Richards, *Village Life in America 1852–1872*

108. Detail—Basket; Mary High Prince and others; Bedford County, Tennessee; c. 1863; pieced and appliquéd cotton. Photograph courtesy Hearts and Hands Media Arts, San Francisco. (Collection of Emeline P. Gist) This quilt was one of many made and raffled by Confederate women during the Civil War to raise money for their cause. One of the signers, Mary High, later married a Confederate soldier, Benjamin Prince, whose name also appears on the quilt. An inscription on the quilt reads: "In evry Object that hear [sic] I see,/ Some of my Friends seem to point at me,/ Love of Friends can never cease,/ In time of War in time of peace."

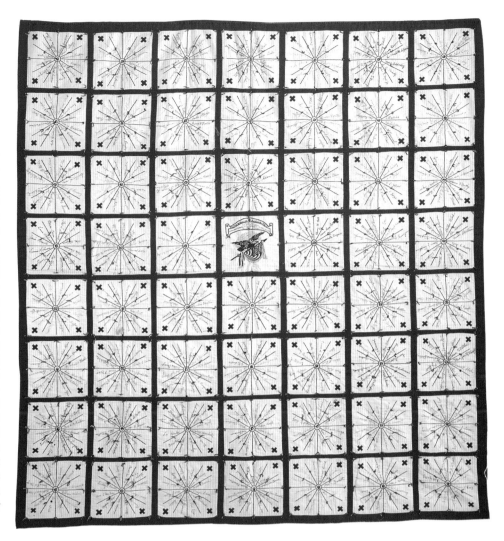

109. Red Cross Quilt; made by
members of the Putnam Valley
Auxiliary No. 1; Putnam Valley,
New York; 1917–1918; pieced and
embroidered cotton; 89″ x 76″.
Photograph by Scott Bowron
courtesy New York Quilt Project,
Museum of American Folk Art,
New York City. (Collection of
Putnam County Historical Society, Gift of Mrs. Rundel Gilbert)
This tied quilt was made during
World War I and, with well over
600 signatures inked between the
radiating spokes on the blocks, it
very likely helped to raise several
hundred dollars for Putnam Valley Auxiliary No. 1. It was not
unusual for fundraising quilts
made during World Wars I and II
to carry nationalistic insignia such
as eagles and flags, and this quilt
is no exception. The red crosses
stitched at the corners of each
block emphasize the cause for
which it was made.

110. Dachau Quilt; former prisoners of a satellite camp of
Dachau; Dachau, Germany; 1945; pieced wools and cotton;
77″ x 70″. (Courtesy America Hurrah Antiques, New York City)
A simple but poignant piece made of men's suiting fabrics, this
quilt serves as a potent reminder of war and its atrocities. The
quilt was brought back from Europe by Lt. Col. Henry Roach,
45th Division of the U.S. Army, who had administered Dachau
for a period after its liberation. It is thought that the quilt may
have been made for him, possibly by the former inmates of
Landsburg, one of Dachau's three satellite camps, where there
were workshops with sewing machines. The fabrics in the quilt
are mostly from the 1930s and were most probably scraps left
over after clothes stored by the Nazis were recut and used to
outfit liberated prisoners on their way to Displaced-Persons'
camps.

Hoorah! for the homespun
dresses we southern ladies
wore in time of the war.
Ev'ry piece here.
Sad memories it brings
back to me.
For our hearts was weary
and restless.
And our life was full of care.
The burden laid up on us
seemed greater than we could bear.

The thousands of quilts made as part of the war-relief effort by women on both sides were crucial contributions, but they did more than provide needed and useful items from which their menfolk would benefit, either directly or indirectly. They furnished a means of therapy for the women who worked on them, an outlet for sharing the stress, worry, and grief under which they labored while their husbands, lovers, sons, and brothers fought a long and difficult war. After the war, women continued to make quilts to benefit former soldiers and their families on both sides, and to find mutual healing and comfort in working together to counteract both the physical and psychological devastation of the war years.

World War I focused women's sights once more on war relief. Although less ill-prepared than at the time of the Civil War, the unexpected length of the war and the massive number of men involved severely taxed government resources, and women once more stepped forward to contribute their share. Through Red Cross–initiated activities as well as in numerous church and lay groups around the country, women again joined together to produce clothing and bedding, to roll material for bandages, and to raise money for supplies. The federal government itself recognized the usefulness of this still largely silent resource and urged women to make quilts. As the war neared its end, slogans and other exhortations such as "Make quilts—save the blankets for our boys over there" were commonly appearing in magazines and newspapers throughout the country, and women responded by the thousands.[10] Red Cross Signature quilts were especially popular as fundraisers, and several women's magazines gave specific guidelines for making them or included articles encouraging them.[11] Although quilting, except in rural areas, was a fading art in many parts of the country at the time, many women were induced to try their hand at it as a part of the war effort and, in the process, found that they forged friendships and developed skills that would long survive the war.

Women took war-relief efforts beyond provisions for soldiers only in this war. The benevolent tradition was now firmly entrenched, and some church groups, especially

those whose philosophies were strongly pacifist, looked beyond the battlefields to the needs of those displaced and suffering as a result of war and made quilts for their use.[12] World War II saw virtually no quilts made as a part of a war-supply effort, but women made thousands for the relief of refugees and other displaced persons. The Relief Society of the Mormon Church, which had had a quiltmaking program for the needy since 1842, was especially involved at this time; such work was considered a personal and moral responsibility, and estimates are that close to 40,000 quilts were made by this group for donation to European needy after the war.[13] Fundraisers were also made, although not to the extent that they had been made for prior wars. The Women's International Bowling Congress was one group that played a large part in the fundraising effort—an Army Air Force bomber was named "Miss WIBC" in its honor due to the money the WIBC had raised—and one fundraising quilt that a chapter of that group is known to have made even depicts a bomber![14] Many other groups that made fundraising quilts during World War II also chose to use patriotic motifs, whether or not the goal was directly a part of the war effort; the implicit statement of allegiance served to ensure enthusiastic participation in the project, whether as a contributor of skill, time, or money.

One of the most memorable quilts known to have been created in response to the events of World War II is the Dachau quilt, for its very simplicity and fabrics serve as a poignant reminder of the atrocities that occurred there. This quilt was made by men and, perhaps, helped them to put to rest some of the ghosts of the past as they worked together on a project to honor one of the liberators of their camp.[15] Other quilts made during this war were Presentation or Friendship pieces for soldiers, and they, too, often carried patriotic reminders, such as the mention of Pearl Harbor in the Crazy quilt shown in figure 111. These quilts served both to commemorate the soldier's role in the war and to allow those on the home front to express their recognition of and pride in his contribution to his country.

Patriotic expressions of recognition and support during time of war have remained very much a part of the vocabulary of quilters in America through the years. During the Gulf War in 1990, for example, many groups produced quilts expressing their endorsement of and support for the U. S. position on Iraq. One of the more interesting efforts was carried out by the On-Line Quilters Guild, which developed a project in which a group of quilters swapped patriotic blocks that they had made and then made quilts from them. Although each quilt contained the same blocks, no two quilts looked alike, for each quilter followed her own creative drive in putting them together! The resulting quilts were shown at

111. Crazy; Anna J. E. Duryee and friends; Kingston, New York; 1942; pieced and embroidered satins, corduroy, velvet, taffeta, mesh, lace, cotton, ribbon; 62″ x 46″. Photograph by J. Breger. (Private collection) This quilt was made as a presentation gift during World War II. It is thought to have been organized by Anna Duryee, whose name appears on the quilt, for her fiancé, a soldier, or possibly a sailor. The quilt has many references to the war, including the embroidered notation "Remember Pearl Harbor." A number of other names appear (presumably friends or relatives of the fiancé), along with several endearments, Christian crosses and Stars of David, and what is probably a fraternity insignia. The date, "Jan 14 1917," might well be the birth date of the man for whom this was made.

112. Stars and Stripes Forever; Diane Rode Schneck; New York, New York; 1992; cottons, cotton blends; 64¾" x 74". Photograph by Karen Bell. (Collection of and © Diane Rode Schneck) During the Gulf War in 1991, twenty-six quilters from the On-line Quilters Guild (a group that keeps in contact through GEnie—the General Electric Network for Information Exchange—decided to relieve some of their anxiety about the war by exchanging quilt blocks with a patriotic theme. Each member chose a pattern and theme fabrics and made a block for every other woman in the exchange; each was then free to combine the block she received into a quilt of her own design. The final combination of blocks made every quilt unique. In addition, because many of the participating women had grown to admire the leadership style of General Norman Schwartzkopf during the Desert Storm Operation, they decided to make a companion quilt for him, also composed of blocks provided by the participants, as a sign of their respect and admiration.

113. National Peace Quilt; Boise Peace Quilt Project; 1984; pieced, appliquéd, and embroidered cottons and cotton blends; 106″ x 116″. Photograph © Boise Peace Quilt Project, Boise, Idaho. This quilt, which represents children's visions of peace and security, contains a block from every state in the Union. Each U.S. senator has been asked to sleep under the quilt and then have his or her name embroidered on it. The legend on the quilt says it all:

> REST beneath the warmth and weight of our hopes
>   for the future of our children,
> DREAM a vision of a world at peace,
> ACT to give the vision life.

114. Campaign Flag Quilt; made by Young family members; Pennsylvania; c. 1844; pieced cotton; 84″ x 76″. Photograph courtesy Kentucky Historical Society, Frankfort, Kentucky. (Collection of The Old Barracks Museum, Trenton, New Jersey) This quilt was made for the Presidential campaign of 1844, when Henry Clay, in his third and final (and unsuccessful) try at the presidency, ran with Theodore Frelinghuysen on the Whig Party ticket. The body of the quilt is made of banners produced for the campaign, and it is possible that the outer border was a later addition. Such banners were easily available and were favorites to include in quilts as an expression of opinion and position. The black fabric apparently was added to reinforce the ties, and the white areas are conservation repairs.

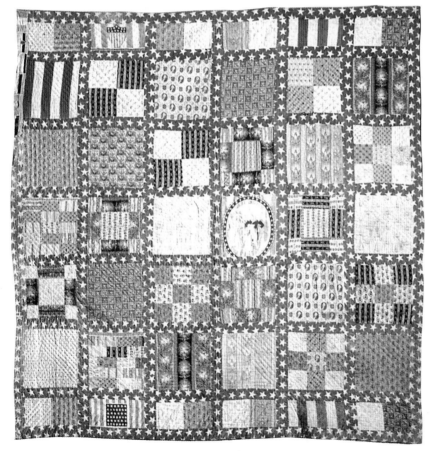

115. Bradbury Centennial Quilt; Emily and Harriet Bradbury and Maria Silsby; Charleston, New Hampshire; 1876; pieced cotton; 87″ x 78″. (Collection of The Smithsonian Institution, Washington, D.C.; Gift of Mrs. C. A. Rich) The quilt, a classic example of one created to celebrate the founding of the nation, is made of samples of commemorative fabrics collected by Mr. Bradbury, a dry-goods merchant in New York City who would have had access to all the newest fabrics of the time. The quilt, which includes roller-printed banners and kerchiefs (see, for example, the block showing George Washington standing with his horse), as well as dress fabrics, was put together by Mr. Bradbury's wife Emily, their twelve-year-old daughter Harriet, and her grandmother, Maria Silsby. Motifs include portraits of George and Martha Washington and Lafayette, eagles, flags, Liberty caps, muskets, cannonballs, liberty bells, and the dates 1776–1876. The quilt is backed in the star-covered blue fabric that was used as sashing on the front, and banners or kerchiefs showing George and Martha Washington, the Declaration of Independence, and the flags and coats of arms of many nations.

Decatur House in Washington, D.C., in 1992 as a tribute to this far-flung grass-roots expression of support to the troops overseas.

Several quilt projects have been devoted to peace and disarmament in an effort to help people cope with global issues that are of a scale beyond what the individual or family can hope to deal with, and which create a wave of frustration or fear in their wake. The Boise Peace Project, which involved hundreds of women, men, and children here and in the former Soviet Union in making dozens of quilts to symbolize a lasting commitment to world peace and friendship, oversaw the creation of the National Peace Quilt, which contains blocks from all fifty states. Every member of the United States Senate was asked to sleep at least one night beneath "the warmth and weight of our hopes for the future of our children," the words that are embroidered on this quilt. The Peace Ribbon was a project that ultimately drew together thousands of submissions from around the world that were stitched together end to end until they formed a "ribbon" eighteen and one-half miles long that was tied around the Pentagon on August 4, 1985, as a symbol of peace and hope encircling a symbol of war. Although today the fading of the cold war has brought with it a lessening of the fears that led to the creation of the Boise Project and the Peace Ribbon, should the need arise again, there is no doubt that women will once more take up needle and thread—ever a symbol of home, life, and hope—to make themselves heard as loudly through their stitches as through their words.

Although wars and their aftermath have undoubtedly resulted in many of the most emotionally stirring and dramatically inscribed examples of patriotic sentiments receiving a voice through quilts, women have also used their needlework to express their national beliefs and loyalties at other times as well. Elections have always caused a swell of enthusiastic response, and, even though for many years women did not have the right to vote, they could not be stopped from voting with their needles, fabric, and thread. Campaign kerchiefs and banners frequently found their way into quilts, creating statements of preference on the part of the makers that would often long outlive the candidate of choice.

Significant national anniversaries, such as the 1876 Centennial Exposition in Philadelphia and the 1976 Bicentennial Celebration, resulted in an explosion of commemorative quilts with patriotic themes, many of them done by groups. The Centennial celebration gave birth to an extensive variety of printed yard goods that incorporated patriotic images, national heroes (George Washington was, of course, a favorite), a ubiquitous red, white, and blue color scheme, and a host of other nationalistic themes, and women quickly incorporated these fabrics into many of the quilts made to commemorate this event. Quilts that did not incorporate the signature fabrics often included pieced or appliquéd blocks showing scenes of historic significance, such as Independence Hall in Philadelphia.

By the time of the Bicentennial, quiltmaking was at a low ebb in this country, but this event served as the spark for numerous women to look once again at the core values and skills that made this country what it is, and quilting became a "rediscovered" art. The burst of patriotic sentiment that surrounded the Bicentennial may also have had some of its roots in the need for healing that followed the bitter years of the Vietnam conflict, and the nation's 200th anniversary provided an ideal opportunity for this to occur. Whatever the reasons, the quilts made in conjunction with the Bicentennial shine with patriotism and love of country, and many who otherwise would not have considered themselves quilters joined together to produce fitting tributes to this landmark event. The 1986 centennial anniversary of the Statue of Liberty, an enduring symbol for this country since its installation, also encouraged the creation of an outstanding group of patriotic quilts, many of them made in response to a competition sponsored by the Museum of American Folk Art in New York City.[16]

The examples given here are only a few of the many instances in which American women have chosen to express their patriotism through their needles, leaving us lasting and cogent reminders that sentiments may be voiced in more than one compelling way. These quilts also represent the combined efforts of women—and men—who joined their skills and their thoughts in cooperative and often eloquent efforts to express their commitment to and belief in the national ideals of their times.

101

116. Centennial Album; Members of the Burdick-Childs family; North Adams, Massachusetts; 1876–1880s; appliquéd cotton; 78½" x 79¾". Photograph by Ken Burris. (Collection of Shelburne Museum, Shelburne, Vermont) The blocks in this quilt depicting Independence Hall and banners reading "Declaration of Independence...Centennial Anniversary...1776–1876" reflect the interest generated throughout the country by the Centennial celebrations of 1876, while others reflect the more homely concerns of the makers, leavened by a lively sense of humor ("My first proposal," "My last proposal," and "The Tiresome Boy"). Several of the more elaborate blocks appear to have been designed and made by the same person, while others were produced by less skilled hands.

117. Putnam County Quilt; nineteen makers, designed by Gladys Boalt, © 1976; Putnam Valley, New York; 1976; pieced, appliquéd, and embroidered cotton; 108″ x 86″. (Private collection) This Bicentennial quilt encapsulates the history of Putnam County, New York, from the eighteenth to the twentieth century. It is a lively and colorful cornucopia of information, a wonderful history lesson delivered with verve and skill, encompassing daily scenes and activities along with nature's delights. The extraordinary amount of detail and the overlapping and intertwined elements that comprise the work required a high degree of cooperation from the quilt's nineteen makers. Its designer, Gladys Boalt, notes that "It is the nature of women to work well together most of the time," and it is clear that this collective ability contributed to the success of this spectacular Bicentennial undertaking.

118. Great Quilt block by Ralph and Shanna Goings. Ralph Goings, a painter in the Photorealist style, was creating a series of truck paintings at the time the quilt was done, and he and his wife used a prototype from his work as the focal point of their block.

119. *Blue-Chip Pick-Up*; Ralph Goings; 1969; oil on canvas; 45″ x 52″. Photograph courtesy O.K. Harris Gallery, New York City. (Private collection)

120. The Great Quilt; Marilynn Karp (coordinator), Regina Wickham (assembler), and others; New York, New York; 1972; pieced, appliquéd, and embroidered cotton, velvet, felt, paint and rhoplex, sequins, metal studs, other mixed media; 94″ x 75″. Photograph courtesy O.K. Harris Gallery, New York City. (Collection of Jessie N. Karp) Many people became much more aware of quilts in the early and mid 1970s, in great part due to the resurgence of interest in colonial crafts that preceded the American Bicentennial in 1976. Marilynn Karp, an artist, responded to the quilt revival by getting people in the graphic arts interested in a quilting project. "The Bicentennial seemed the most logical theme," she notes, and interested artists connected with her husband's O.K. Harris Gallery in SoHo, as well as relatives and friends were each asked to make a 12″ x 12″ block in red, white, and blue. Some blocks reflected the artists' subject matter (see detail and painting); others reflected general interest; still others were created just for fun. Some of the artists who helped to create the quilt are Richard Artschwager, Richard Estes, David Diao, Ralph Goings, Richard Pettibone, James Wines, Allison Sky, Martin Hoffman, and Richard Friedberg.

121. Detail—Crazy; made for the Grist family by members of the East Troupsburg Church Sewing Circle; Troupsburg, New York; 1912; cotton, wool; 81″ x 70″. Photograph courtesy New York Quilt Project, Museum of American Folk Art, New York City. (Collection of Roy Grist) This quilt carries the name of a number of the members of the Grist family on it, but the most intriguing block is one that carries the legend "Ray Towsley killed by a log Feb 20 1912." The family clearly felt strongly enough about this family member to want to keep his memory alive. The quilt was put together by a church sewing circle and may have been made in recognition of this loss.

"I Will Remember Thee"

"Think not though distant thou art
Thou cannot forgotten be
While memory lives within my heart
I will remember thee."[1]

"...the custom of mourning presses far more heavily on women than
men...practically the whole burden...would seem to have fallen on
women....[The men] positively manage to mourn by proxy!"[2]

Death was very much a constant companion in preceding centuries; it might often be sudden, but it was never unexpected. Plague, accident, illness, infant mortality, and violence, coupled with a lack of adequate medical care and none of the drugs that we take for granted today, all combined to give a life expectancy of only forty-five years in 1870.[3] Yet, death's tenacious presence did not make its acceptance any easier.

In preindustrial America, when the total population of the United States stood at fewer than five million, the loss of one person could touch the lives of an entire community, and it was essential to the well-being of the group to repair the rent in the social fabric as rapidly as possible. In Colonial times, people took a pragmatic approach to death; mourning was simple and circumscribed, and a funeral provided a clear-cut closing that allowed the living, after turning to each other to express community solidarity and support as they said good-bye, to move on to the unfinished business of life. The move toward industrialization with the dawn of the nineteenth century decreased the social interdependence of the seventeenth and eighteenth centuries, however, and the "emotional revolution" that accompanied the advent of Romanticism placed the funeral as the beginning rather than the end point of mourning; it also laid the burden of death more heavily on the individual and family rather than disbursing it throughout the community.[4] Mourning rituals became rigid and unbending, reaching their apogee with Queen Victoria's intense, dedicated, and prolonged mourning for her husband and her mother at mid-century. Yet, for all their apparent preeminence, rigid mourning customs were essentially a bourgeois phenomenon; the poor could ill afford to indulge in the time, effort, and trappings required for the "proper" acknowledgment of death and loss.

Given the ideology of the "woman's sphere" (prevalent by the 1830s), which attributed natures more pious, sentimental, and emotional to women than to men, it followed that women would bear the brunt of the nineteenth-century romantic attitude toward death, and they became guardians not only of the hearth, but of the grave. But while the peculiar attributes of the woman's sphere might sometimes seem to place an intolerable responsibility on women, it also offered an excuse for interaction with and the understanding of their peers, who labored under the same constraints. Just as women could call on a system of mutual aid in childbirth and illness, so too would they rally together to share the burden of loss and mourning, as can be seen in many of the diaries and journals of earlier times:

When I was about four years old the neighbor's baby died, and all the women was called in to help. Mama knew what her part was because right away she took some blue silk out of her hope chest. I remember that silk so well because it was special and I got to carry it. When we got to the neighbors some of the women was cooking and the men was making the casket. Mama and three other women set up the frame and quilted all day. First they quilted the lining for the casket, and then they made a tiny little quilt out of the blue silk to cover the baby.[5]

I got up at half past five and found Mrs. Ketchum up to Mrs. Ward's. Their baby sickened and died. She helped lay it out, then came home to breakfast....Two ladies came in and helped make a shroud for the Baby.[6]

At a time of loss, quilting provided an escape as well as a means of coping with grief. A woman could take refuge in a familiar chore of everyday life, using it as an avenue of comfort; through it, she could take advantage of the support system of her female friends, relatives, and neighbors, joining with them in a socially acceptable project that allowed expressions of grief and sympathy to meld and merge while creating a tangible reminder of the loved one. Mourning or memorial quilts were a step in the healing process, a stitch in the rip of the social fabric that death caused. Like those quilts made for friends and relatives about to depart for a new life, be it through marriage or on the frontier, mourning and memory quilts

122. Sampler; makers unknown; Canton, Ohio; c. 1888; pieced, appliquéd, and embroidered cotton; size unavailable. Photograph courtesy Laura Fisher/Antique Quilts and Americana, New York City. (Private collection) Whatever the actual reason may be for the creation of this quilt, it certainly was made by many hands, and several blocks appear to have been made as a memorial; one includes the embroidered words "A stranger, A friend" and "I have suffered." The possibility of the quilt's having been made as a memorial is underscored by the signature of a Reverend Loveback. The mystery of the quilt is heightened by the inclusion of several national flags—those of the United States, Egypt, Germany, and one inscribed in Arabic.

123a. Detail, with Eli Lilly's signature.
Photograph courtesy Gail Treschel.

123. Album; made by family and friends of Eli Lilly; Baltimore, Maryland; 1847; appliquéd cotton; 106″ x 106″. Photograph by Karen Bell. (Collection of Louise Francke) The family of Eli Lilly gathered from near and far away (some had moved as far as Independence, Missouri) to carry out a bedside vigil during the months of the patriarch's final illness and made the blocks for this quilt as they comforted their father and each other. Family history has it that one daughter was not present because she was too advanced in pregnancy to make the long journey from Missouri to Baltimore, but her husband came in her place. The quilt is signed by nine of Lilly's eleven children, their spouses, and several friends; Lilly himself signed the block with the lyre, a symbol of mourning. The laurel wreath (first row, right) and the drooping tulips (second row, left) may also be intended as symbols of mourning. The blocks were collected and kept by Minerva Ann Lilly, a daughter who had not yet married and was still living at home (her block is the center one in the bottom row). It is thought that she is the one who later joined and quilted the blocks, perhaps with some help from other family members. In 1851, Minerva married Benjamin Crowther, who, during the Civil War, was a member of Shelby's regiment, a Confederate group that refused to surrender at the end of the Civil War. These soldiers and their families then went to Mexico and settled in Carlota, in Vera Cruz. Minerva carried the quilt with her to Mexico and later to San Antonio, where she moved after her husband's death, thus preserving a priceless bit of family history. One of Eli Lilly's grandsons was the founder of the present-day Lilly Pharmaceutical Company.

served the purpose of a ceremonial leavetaking, a way of saying good-bye, a fitting outlet for both silent and verbal expression of the pain and anguish of separation.

Mourning quilts were often made from the clothing of the deceased. One quilt, known as the "shroud quilt" or "coffin quilt," made by Polly Taylor and Elizabeth Taylor Ruff in memory of Polly's husband, a soldier, includes remnants of his clothes as well as pieces of the casket lining; names of other family members, some with birth and death dates, further enhance the memorial aspect of this quilt. Mourning clothes worn by the living might be incorporated into such a quilt as well—one woman is known to have used her mourning coat in a quilt made in memory of her husband.[7] In this century, ribbons from funeral floral offerings are also known to have been used in quilts, although, according to Treschel, such usage seems to occur more often in rural than urban communities.[8]

Many of the quilts made by groups to honor the dead are Album and Signature quilts, and there is evidence to suggest that Quaker groups found such quilts of particular value to make.[9] The inscriptions that appeared on these Signature quilts were often similar to those that appeared on the Friendship quilts made for those leaving the community, although in the case of mourning quilts the sentiment "Remember Me" may have been meant as a plea to the dead person to remember the living when in heaven as well as an evocation of the memory of him or her. However, more dramatic and final sentiments were often expressed, and references to funerals, death, and graves were common.

One quite beautiful quilt of the Baltimore Album type was made by the family of Eli Lilly in 1847, and the dying man himself participated in its making. According to family tradition, many members of the family gathered together during Lilly's final weeks and made the blocks for the quilt at his bedside. Work on the quilt provided a reason for the family to gather together physically and to prepare spiritually and emotionally for their patriarch's death.[10] Today, a similar pattern is followed by some victims of AIDS, who work with friends on their own memorial panels that will become part of the NAMES Project AIDS Memorial Quilt after their death.

Because women were no less susceptible to death than men—the chances of surviving childbirth alone were not negligible in the nineteenth century[11]—a quilt begun by one woman might often be completed by others as a lasting token of friendship, love, and esteem. The women who picked up the broken threads might be family members or intimate friends. Sometimes a husband's new wife would complete the project that her predecessor had begun, either through a dislike of waste or a desire to fulfill perceived familial obligations—or, perhaps, the recognition that someday someone might be perpetuating her memory by carrying out a similar chore. Thus,

women's support of and dependence on each other at times could transcend even death.

One such quilt is both a eulogy to the young girl who started it and an indication of the affection in which she was held by her family and friends, most especially by her stepmother. Laura Mahan died in 1848 at the tender age of fourteen, when a quilt she had begun was far from complete. Her stepmother, Sarah, had become deeply attached to Laura and decided to finish her quilt, ensuring in this way that a beloved child would not be forgotten. Thus, Sarah created a glowing tribute to her stepdaughter's memory as well as a means of coping with her own grief. That the quilt would also be an ongoing bond of love for the family was made clear by a label that Sarah stitched to its back:

> This quilt, begun by our dear Laura & finished by me, principally from fragments of her dresses, I give & bequeath to her sister Julia M. Woodruff, or in case of her death to her sister Hila M. Hall, if she survives, or otherwise to the oldest surviving granddaughter of their father, Artemas Mahan, deceased.—Sarah Mahan/Oberlin Feb. 6, 1851.

The forty-five blocks in the quilt—many made from Laura's own clothes—are inscribed by family members and friends with biblical quotations and contemporary sentimental verses, providing a true testament of community.[12]

In some cases, rather than dedicating an entire quilt to a loved one, one or more blocks might be included as reminders of those who had gone. Sometimes simply the fabrics of which the blocks were made were enough to stir the memory and keep former bonds alive: "I remember one fragment in particular...a delicate sea moss pattern, a fragment of a dress belonging to my dead sister. When I looked at it, I always saw her face before me."[13] And a swatch of fabric stirred memories at a 1974 family quilting bee in Louisiana: "Boy, I'll tell y'all what. This black and white checkered diamonds is something else to try to do!" "Oh, that's Aunt Dee's. It was something to sew! Lord!" "The black checked?" "Oh, I had a dress out of that." "Oh, I did too."[14]

Anonymous blocks related to mourning are often found on many Album type quilts as well. There are numerous examples of representations of weeping willows, monuments or catafalques, mourning urns, mourning wreaths, drooping flowers, even coffins and gravestones—symbols of great meaning to those in mourning and ones seen frequently in the mourning art of the nineteenth century—appearing on quilts, but unless an inscription accompanies the block there is rarely enough information to tell us today whether these symbols were in fact an expression of mourning for a specific individual or whether the women who stitched them were simply

124. Chimney Sweep; makers' names unknown; Dryden, New York; 1846–1902; pieced cotton; 88″ x 70″. Photograph by Scott Bowron, courtesy New York Quilt Project, Museum of American Folk Art, New York City. (Collection of Julie Clemens) The Chimney Sweep block, whether set on point or straight as shown here, was one of the most popular of the repetitive patterns used for Signature quilts. The central cross in each block, usually made of unbleached muslin, was ideal to frame a name or a longer inscription. Although the original purpose of this quilt is unclear, many of the blocks contain memorial verses and death dates along with the names. The wide spread of dates may indicate that the blocks were made and collected over nearly half a century, or, more likely, that a group of friends made the blocks for one of their number somewhere around the mid-century, and that the recipient (or a relative) filled in death dates as time went on. The ink is evenly faded now, even for the more recent inscriptions.

incorporating the popular icons of their time into their work.

In other quilts, however, blocks spell out specifically those whom they honor. Several blocks in a quilt from upstate New York contain memorial verses (similar to those that appeared on samplers earlier in the century), often with a name, death date, and age:

But death the early reaper, he
Who ever plucks the fairest flowers
Has been among us, Stolen the(e)
And borne the(e) from this world of ours.
    Almira Fitts, Died
    October 8[the] 1842

    C.C. Hurd
    Died Oct
    11[the] 1845
She has gone to the mansion of rest,
From a region of sorrow and pain
To the glorious land of the blessed
Where she never can suffer again.
    Aged 25 years
    1 month
    7 days

Another family quilt made near the beginning of this century, for the most part a lively presentation of names of many family members, has one block that carries a grim message and reminder of the suddenness of death: "Ray Towsley killed by a log Feb 20 1912." Quilts such as these latter two often serve, intentionally or not, as a sort of family or community genealogical guide, whereby both the living and the dead are recognized as having their rightful and recognized places in the community.

Women worked together on quilts not only to honor family and friends but also to memorialize public figures and to express in a more personal way the esteem and respect in which they were held. Many such quilts were made following the assassination of Abraham Lincoln; one of those created in his honor even incorporated some black mourning crepe that had been used to decorate the State House in Indianapolis, Indiana.[15] The turn of the century saw a tribute to the assassinated President McKinley in the hundreds, if not thousands, of "penny squares" pre-stamped with his portrait and then embroidered and incorporated into quilts around the country. Other quilts included blocks as memorials to a well-known person; the Washington Monument (in Baltimore), for example, was a favorite for inclusion on quilts of the Baltimore Album type. War heroes were other favorites for memorialization, and blocks honoring

two heroes of the War with Mexico, Major Samuel Ringgold and Colonel William H. Watson, both of whom were killed in action in 1846, are known from several Baltimore quilts.[16]

This century has moved away from the often extravagant displays of grief and mourning that played so large a part in the ritual of grief of the Victorian era, yet loss today is no less real and leaves a void that must be filled. Many contemporary quilters have found that quilting can still provide the comfort so necessary and important to those who are grieving, that it remains an aid to the healing process, that the creation of these tangible memorials underscores the old adage that "a burden shared is a burden halved." Today, these quilts may often be private expressions of a personal and local loss, shared only by those who knew the deceased, but other times a public tragedy has so touched the imagination and lives of many that an outlet for the emotions created is imperative. The January 28, 1986, Challenger disaster was such an event; and quilters across the country created testimonials to the grief and loss felt by a nation.[17] The AIDS epidemic, a cumulation of individual public and private anguish, is another.

The AIDS Memorial Quilt, created by those who lost friends, spouses, lovers, parents, children, or siblings to AIDS, carries not only personal and public manifestations of grief and mourning, but also a message about an issue that has touched the lives of so many. It is indeed a memorial quilt, but it is a quilt of conscience as well, reminding all who see it not only of the lives that AIDS has taken but also of the fact that neither the disease nor the problems associated with it have disappeared, an ever-growing reminder of a problem still to be solved. And, though it is the largest and best-known, it is not the only quilt that is now being used as a mechanism to raise public consciousness about tragic issues. Others, for example, include quilts made by members of MADD (Mothers Against Drunk Driving), which have served both as memorials to children who were victims of drunk drivers and to bring public attention to the problem as well as to the goals of the organization. The Dachau quilt is a poignant reminder of man's inhumanity to his fellows, and quilts made to commemorate the victims of Hiroshima and Nagasaki also serve to remind the world of the destructive capabilities of the atomic bomb. These are only a few of the areas in which quilters have found not only outlets for the expression of their emotions but also opportunities to raise public awareness and the ability to act in the hope that one day in the future, although death will still be with us, its occurrence from these causes at least will be only a memory.

125. Detail—Basket; Mary High Prince and others; Bedford County, Tennessee; c. 1863; pieced and appliquéd cotton; 74″ x 96″. Photograph courtesy Tennessee Quilt Project, Chattanooga, Tennessee. (Collection of Emeline P. Gist) The blocks of this Basket quilt, made and raffled by Confederate women during the Civil War to raise money for their cause, were made by or dedicated to different people. This Basket was dedicated to the memory of Capt. P.B. Anderson, a soldier who had lost his life fighting for the Confederate cause. The inscription under the handle of the Basket reads: "TV [probably shorthand for Tennessee Volunteer] Dec'd./He went to rest/In all his country's honors drest."

126. Detail—Steven Salamone panel for the AIDS Memorial Quilt; made by friends and relatives; Woodside, New York; 1992. Photograph by Karen Bell courtesy Metro New York Quilters.

127. *Ode to J.L., Queen of the Bronx*; thirteen members of the Empire Quilters Guild; New York; 1990; cotton; 57″ x 54″. Photograph courtesy Marilyn Henrion. This quilt, completed and now owned by Marilyn Henrion, resulted from a block challenge among members of the Empire Quilters Guild. The challenge was to create a setting for the thirteen otherwise unrelated blocks, each made by a different quilter. Marilyn created frames for those blocks and then made some unfilled frames to represent quilters of the past "in whose footsteps we follow." The title of the quilt refers to Judy Lynne-Peters, organizer of the challenge.

The More of You There Are

"It's more fun the more of you there are."[1]

"...this group of ladies taught me how to bring up kids, how to be a good wife, how to cook!—they were there! They have supported me forever. Now I'm one of the older ones but...I NEED THEM."[2]

Belonging to a group spurs you on to do more....Everyone is helpful and encouraging and warm and kind. When you hit a snag and can't create anything—a quilt group is just what you need."[3]

"We truly enjoy being together...."[4]

The years leading up to the 1976 Bicentennial helped to usher in a new era in quilting, as women began to look backward to rediscover their roots as well as the joy of joining together in a new "old" activity. Women who shared a common interest in this traditional activity formed groups or guilds for the purpose of learning more or to foster a greater appreciation of it, and, in the course of learning more about quilting, they learned more about themselves and others as well. The groups became important because of the pervasive sense of friendship, sharing, and mutual support as well as for their stated purposes of quilting.

The surge of interest sparked by the Bicentennial saw quilting moved from its perception as something only rural ladies in church-aid societies did to something that garnered national attention and respect. As a result, an unprecedented number of guilds and groups of all sizes (the larger, regional ones are composed of a variety of smaller local groups) were formally established around the country, and their growth in the last twenty years has been nothing short of remarkable. Many of their members may have originally joined as part of the revival movement, but they have remained because of the sense of community and group identity that participation in a group promotes. As more than one woman has said, "you're never a stranger" at a quilt group; whatever differences there may be in social, economic, educational, or ethnic terms, the common bond of quilting ties the group into a cohesive and supportive whole as personal and social relations become inseparable from the quiltmaking experience.[5] Quilting has never recognized boundaries; the very nature of the activity demands mutual cooperation and respect. Many quilting groups, on a voluntary basis, have done painlessly what is still being achieved with only a good deal of effort nationally—racial integration.[6]

Today, as yesterday, the desire for companionship and

sharing has also played its part in bringing people into a group, and many have found quilt groups to be somewhat reminiscent of the consciousness-raising groups of the 1960s and 1970s: "[It was a] chance to escape and share what it meant to us to be wives and mothers and women—and the quilting was important, too."[7] Helen Grigg, a quilter, designer, and one of organizers of the Northwest Quilters, says that what happens over quilts with a group of women is important: "There is great bonding. This is where they share their lives."[8] The bottom line is that women know the other women are there—the support group is available if anyone is in need.

Not all sewing and quilting groups are new; there are many, often affiliated with churches, that have been active, in one form or another, for scores of years, although some are suffering today as the younger women of a parish often prefer a less stereotyped setting and join a guild or other nondenominational group if they wish to be involved in quilting. And not all guilds grew out of the 1970s—many have been active for fifty years or more. Some were logical developments of church-related ladies'-aid or missionary societies; others grew from women with common interests in sewing and quilting who wanted a way to meet regularly and share a mutual pleasure as well as the concerns of the day. A fictional quilt club that formed the basis of the Nancy Page newspaper column from 1925 to 1940 also served as the inspiration for many real ones and provided a basis on which later clubs could be built.[9] Whether old or new, however, the motivation for joining these groups has seemed to be much the same over the years—friendship, sharing, and support.[10]

The old adage, "the more things change, the more they stay the same," might apply equally well to group quilting today. Women now gather together to make quilts for many of the same reasons they always did—to raise money for favored causes, to help those in need, to give

128. *The Judy Quilt*; Judith Berlo Tucker, Judy Walker, Judy Klein, Judy Dales, Judy Doenias, Judy Hopkins, Judy Anne Walter, Judy Speezak, Judy Lynne-Peters, Judy Fletcher, Judy Ruth, Judy Smith-Kressley, Judy Cohen, Judy Shapiro, Judy Berns, Judy Mathieson, Judy Donovan, Judy Kratts; assembled in Flushing, New York; 1992; pieced and appliquéd cotton and other fabrics; 67″ x 80″. Photograph by Karen Bell courtesy The Quilting Judys. In 1989, at Quilting-by-the-Lake, Flushing, there were so many Judys present that a group called The Quilting Judys was formed. Eighteen of the original twenty members of the group submitted a block for this fun quilt, which was then assembled by Judy Doenias and quilted by Judy Klein. The only condition (other than size) was that each block had to contain a "J" or the name "Judy" on it—and some are very cleverly disguised indeed! (Note the one that says "Judy" with signal flags.) The quilt will be donated to St. Jude's Hospital for Children in Atlanta. The Quilting Judys have continued and expanded (they now number sixty members), and more joint projects are planned.

129. *Edith and Polly*; Variable Star Quilters; Souderton, Pennsylvania; 1990; appliquéd cotton, lace; 72″ x 72″. Photograph by Scott Bowron. (Collection of Museum of American Folk Art, New York City) This quilt was the First Place Grand Prize Winner in the 1991 Friends Sharing America contest sponsored by the Museum of American Folk Art. The contest saw a wide range of entries from groups around the country and was living proof that the tradition of communal quilting is very much alive and well today! The Variable Star Quilters, which draws its membership from an area covering three counties, started in 1978 and has a number of communal projects to its credit, from raffle quilts to the reprinting of a 1941 WPA manual on quilts and quilting. As one member says, "We work well together!" The design of two women exchanging a jar of pickles was chosen, according to the quilters, because they saw sharing—especially of food and conversation—as the basis of friendship.

130. *You Are Precious*; Church of the Resurrection; Michigan; 1992; pieced cotton, cotton blends; 45⅜″ x 39″. Photograph by Karen Bell courtesy ABC Quilts, Brooklyn, New York. This is another of the many crib quilts made for ABC Quilts by groups throughout the U.S. to bring some comfort to children in crisis.

recognition, to create a memorial, to acknowledge friendship, to draw attention to issues and concerns. Today, the funds raised might go to help renovate a national monument such as the Statue of Liberty rather than a church; the needy might be AIDS babies or Ronald McDonald House residents rather than a local indigent family or the Sanitary Commission; the presentation might be to a cultural institution or major political figure rather than the pastor; the memorial might be one small part of the ever-enlarging AIDS Quilt rather than a remembrance token for a family; or the issue might be universal human rights or world peace rather than women's suffrage; but the underlying intent remains much the same. Women's lives are dramatically different today than were their great-great-grandmothers'—or even their grandmothers'. They have options open to them that once could not even be conceived of, yet many have found that a return to the traditional tools of their gender has, by putting them in touch with the strengths of those who have gone before, given them a new kind of power and the chance to be active in new arenas.

The enthusiasm generated by quilting today has also expanded communal quilting beyond the traditional boundaries and many new avenues are open for exploration. On-line quilt guilds encourage the inclusion of women who may never meet face to face yet have their lives touch through their participation in a cooperative project. As quilting becomes a truly international activity, the American concept of working together flows easily around the globe, and there are now quilt groups in countries where the tradition for such work is only in its infancy—but developing rapidly. Quilting together is also being used in education, to teach both skills and the art of cooperative work. And communal quilting has its therapeutic side as well, for it has been used as a mechanism in some senior-citizen groups as a means of retrieving history and gaining a perspective on the past.

Be it for relaxation, reaffirmation, or rejuvenation, this old tradition has taken on a new life and meaning today, and women still respond. The revival of the 1970s is poised to continue into the next century, and women continue to find the simple pleasures of communal activity—whether done face to face or via an on-line network that allows exchanges across a continent, if not the world—supportive, nurturing, inspiring. Working together will not go away.

131. *Memories of Childhood*; made by senior citizens at Senior Neighbors of Chattanooga, Inc., Chattanooga, Tennessee; 1983; appliquéd cotton; size unavailable. Photograph courtesy Bets Ramsey. (Collection of Senior Neighbors of Chattanooga, Inc.) This charming memory quilt depicts scenes from the makers' childhoods and covers many facets of life, from everyday chores to games and pets. Many of the contributors, all of whom were black, had grown up at a time when life was perhaps simpler but hard, for conveniences were few. The quilt, which captures both the joys and the trials (one block shows a house on fire) of childhood, not only served to produce a lasting monument to life as the makers knew it but also provided them the opportunity to draw closer together as a group; it was a wonderful vehicle for reminiscing and informing others about what memories held special meaning for them. (For more information, see Bets Ramsey, "Recollections of Childhood Recorded in a Tennessee Quilt," *Uncoverings* 1983, Vol. 4, 1984, pp. 27–37.)

132. *Friendship Quilt*; various makers; New York and Tokyo; 1985; pieced, appliquéd, and embroidered mixed fabrics and media; size unavailable. Photograph courtesy Kei Kobayashi. (Collection of Bunka Design School, Tokyo) In a hands-across-the-sea expression of friendship, two groups of quilters—one at the New School for Social Research in New York, and the other at the Bunka Design School in Tokyo, Japan—created a tangible bond. The squares were made by the American quilters, who used red, white, and blue as their theme; the circles were created by the Japanese, and each circle becomes a "plate" holding favorite foods because, as one person involved in the project said, "Eating together represents friendship."

133. Visitors look at some of the 20,064 panels that made up the AIDS Memorial Quilt during its display in Washington, D.C., October 1992. Over 400,000 people viewed the Quilt during this exhibition. Photograph by Marc Geller courtesy The NAMES Project, San Francisco, California.

Epilogue

"There's promise in a quilt. It's not a shroud or tombstone. It's so important for people whose greatest enemy is despair."[1]

The AIDS Memorial Quilt, created by the NAMES Project, is quite possibly the largest communal undertaking that will ever be done in quilting. It has also become an all-encompassing icon of communal endeavor in its broadest and most positive sense, and as such, it is worth a closer look. The Quilt has gone far beyond its original homely intent of supplying an outlet for anguish and a tangible source of comfort for a few to providing a national recognition and sharing of loss and regret for lives cut short, be they those of the famous or the anonymous. It has also become a symbol of much-needed public awareness of a yet-unconquered danger.

The Quilt represents both a personal and a national effort, with its many pieces worked on singly and in groups around the country, to create diverse memorials to the tens of thousands of Americans struck down by AIDS. Cleve Jones, the founder of the NAMES Project, began the process in February 1987 as he searched for a way to cope with the grief and rage he felt at the loss of his best friend, who had died of AIDS four months earlier. He found his sorrow and frustration gradually replaced by a sense of resolution and completion as he created a six- by three-foot panel (roughly the size of a coffin) with his friend's name on it, and he felt comforted when he thought of his memorial as a quilt, because, he says, "quilts represent coziness, humanity and warmth...."[2] As people heard about and saw what he had done, they expressed a desire to make panels, too, either for his friend or for others they knew who had died of AIDS, and so the NAMES Project was born. As the Quilt grew, it slowly became clear that it was more than a means of coping with loss; it was also an ideal way to help educate people across the country about AIDS as well as about the need to mourn, the need to turn toward each other and not away: "The Quilt touches something in people that is pure and good. By providing a glimpse of the lives behind the statistics, it will create an extraordinary, dramatic illustration of the magnitude of this epidemic—to the President, to Congress, and to the country. Also, it's a way for survivors to work through their grief in a positive, creative way."[3]

Seeing the Quilt spread out in its ever-growing entirety (it has now been twice displayed in Washington, D.C.; see fig. 144) or as part of smaller local exhibits, whether of only several panels or several hundred, is to become part of a universal human chain that links us intangibly yet indelibly with those whose names we read and remember, whether we knew them or not. The Quilt strikes an immediate susceptible chord in the viewer, not because of its size—it now includes over 20,000 panels, or its beauty, for many of its panels are not beautiful—but because of the anger and grief, the love and the caring, the sorrow and the hope stitched into every inch, because of the implicit paradox of the need to remember and the pain of letting go. The AIDS Quilt can be considered the apex of mourning quilts as well as a reflective statement of a nation's conscience, for it recognizes private tragedy and public concern, individual victims and a society's loss.

As a cooperative work, the Quilt is unparalleled; it presents a vast array of colors and patterns, of diversity and individuality, of the unconscious collaboration of women, men, and children who are often unknown to each other yet who together have created a stunning monument to those for whom they cared. Many panels are laden with the mementoes of a life, from scraps of clothing to favorite objects, while others are starkly simple. Design concepts range from the spiritual to the irreverent, or even a juxtaposition of the two. The Quilt is a tribute on a grand scale to lives lived, whether in happiness or pain, in suffering or in love, in joy or in grief. Above all, the Quilt is a reminder, and not only for those who are remembered or for those who remember: It is a reminder to all who see it not only of the lives that AIDS has taken but also of the fact that more is yet to come, that neither the disease nor the concerns associated with it have disappeared. Yet, for all the particular tragedies that it represents, the Quilt itself is a sign of hope and resilience. Just as its many thousands of panels continue to be joined to create a whole with a meaning far larger than its parts, so, too, does the social fabric shredded by loss begin to join together again, bringing with it a greater understanding and acceptance, if not always peace.

134. Volunteers working on panels for the AIDS Memorial Quilt. Photograph by Pat Seiter courtesy The NAMES Project, San Francisco, California.

135. Volunteers at The NAMES Project headquarters in San Francisco working on panels for the AIDS Memorial Quilt. Photograph by Marc Geller courtesy The NAMES Project, San Francisco, California.

136. *Jerry Tarantola*; made by relatives with the help of Metro New York Quilters for the AIDS Memorial Quilt; Queens, New York; 1992; collaged satin, canvas, felt, braid; 36″ x 72″. Photograph by Karen Bell courtesy Metro New York Quilters. Many of the panels made for AIDS victims include photographs, a visual reminder of so many lives lost in their prime. On this panel, a photo of Jerry Tarantola's Doberman appears as well. His mother recalls that the dog, trained by her son, was absolutely devoted to him; once, when Jerry fell ill in the street, the dog guarded him so well that it had to be tranquilized before ambulance attendants could get near enough to help. Jerry was diagnosed with AIDS in 1987, when public education about the disease was still in its infancy. His mother and sister remember the fear then shown by hospital employees, some of whom didn't even want to be in the same room as Jerry. "I wish," says Mrs. Tarantola, "that people could be more tolerant." She says that he and his sister—older than Jerry by only thirteen months—were "like clones"; his sister was extremely supportive of Jerry throughout the course of his illness, even sleeping in his hospital room during his final hospitalization so that he would not be alone. After this panel was photographed, the family decided to add silver hearts to it as a symbol of how Jerry remains in their thoughts.

137. *David A. Matos*; made by relatives with the help of Metro New York Quilters as part of the AIDS Memorial Quilt; New York, New York; 1992; collaged cotton velveteen, felt; 36″ x 72″. Photograph by Karen Bell courtesy Metro New York Quilters. A quiet and spiritual tribute to a beloved family member, this gentle remembrance carries with it a sense of acceptance and peace.

138. *Steven Salamone*; made by friends and relatives for the AIDS Memorial Quilt, Woodside, New York; 1992; collaged canvas, cotton, lamé, lace, multimedia; 36″ x 72″. Photograph by Karen Bell courtesy Metro New York Quilters. This lively and colorful panel, filled with reminders of favorite things and places, captures the flavor of this young man's life as well as the sorrow felt by his friends and relatives at his loss. Those involved noted that creating the individual pieces of the collage led to many exchanges of happy memories; it was not until they began to stitch the pieces to the base fabric that tears began to come.

139. *Damein Cannon-Grant*; made by Metro New York Quilters as part of the AIDS Memorial Quilt; Bronx, New York; 1992; collaged satin, canvas, felt, multimedia; 36″ x 72″. Photograph by Karen Bell courtesy Metro New York Quilters.

140. *Rasheen Parker-Grant*; made by Metro New York Quilters as part of the AIDS Memorial quilt; Bronx, New York; 1992; collaged satin, canvas, felt, multimedia; 36″ x 72″. Photograph by Karen Bell courtesy Metro New York Quilters.

The panels for these two children, who were victims of AIDS, were made at the request of their foster parent. A Christmas theme was chosen for the younger one because of the date of his death, and it seemed appropriate for the elder as well, as she was born so close to the holiday.

141. *Arturo Rivera*; Bob Wilson and members of Metro New York Quilters; New York, New York; 1992; collaged satin, felt, sequins, lamé; 36″ x 72″. Photograph by Karen Bell courtesy Metro New York Quilters.

142. *Miguel Mendez*; members of Metro New York Quilters; New York, New York; 1992; handpainted cotton, felt; 36″ x 72″. Photograph by Karen Bell courtesy Metro New York Quilters. Not all those who die of AIDS leave behind family and friends to honor their memories; some die in obscurity, with no loved ones at their sides. In an effort to give some posthumous positive recognition to those whose lives may have held only negatives, the Metro New York Quilters have undertaken to provide panels in their memory, and these two panels are representative of many they have made. Bob Wilson, coordinator of the quilters' group, says that often all they have is a name and the date of death provided by a hospice that cares for these people in their last days, and so the makers give free rein to their imagination in creating the panels. Wilson notes that the design for Arturo Rivera was "an idea I had for a long time and was waiting for the right place to use it"; the panel for Miguel Mendez was created and painted by a group of high-school students who often lend their time to this project.

143. *Leo Foy, Jr.*; made by relatives for the AIDS Memorial Quilt; New Jersey; 1992; collaged satin, canvas, cotton, multimedia; 36″ x 72″. Photograph by Karen Bell courtesy Metro New York Quilters. Leo's last letter to his family and friends, written shortly before his death on January 30, 1990, was transcribed and included in his quilt: "I, Leo Foy, would like to say good-bye to my family and friends that I have known over the years. I am survived by my five sisters: Mary Lou, Frances, Sandra, Nancy and Ruth; and my loving parents, Leo and Nancy; and many uncles, aunts, and cousins. In life I gave my best shot when it came to loving and I will always love my family until I see them again. If you are ever in need, just say this prayer and God will help you as He did me: 'Dear God, Grant the serenity to accept the things I cannot change, the strength to change the things I can, and the love and wisdom to know the difference.' God Bless, I love you all. Love, Leo."

144. *(Overleaf)* The 20,064 panels of the AIDS Memorial Quilt displayed on The Mall in Washington, D.C., October 1992. Photograph by Jeff Tinsley courtesy The NAMES Project, San Francisco, California.

Notes

THE TIES THAT BIND

1. Frances Trollope, *Domestic Manners of the Americans*, Donald Smalley, editor (New York: 1949 edition), p. 414.

2. Lilla Day Monroe, as quoted in Johanna L. Stratton, *Pioneer Women: Voices from the Kansas Frontier* (New York: Simon and Schuster, 1981).

3. See, for example, Lynn A. Bonfield, "Diaries of New England Quilters Before 1860," *Uncoverings 1988*, Vol. 9, 1989, pp. 171-197.

4. Although the *Oxford English Dictionary* (Oxford: (Clarendon Press, 1989, 2nd ed.) defines "bee" as American in origin ("In allusion to social character of the insect [orig. in U.S.]: A meeting of neighbors to unite their labors for the benefit of one of their numbers; e.g., as is done still in some parts, when the farmers unite to get in each other's harvests, usually preceded by a word defining purpose of the meeting: as apple-bee, husking-bee, quilting-bee, etc."), the word is thought to have originated in England. Darryl Lyman, in *The Animal Things We Say* (Middle Village, NY: Jonathan David Publishers, Inc., 1983, p. 11) notes an early custom in some parts of England of giving voluntary help to neighbors for particular tasks. Such help was called a *been* or *bean* (variants of the word *boon*) and probably related directly to the Middle English *bene* (boon or prayer). Lyman believes the custom was carried to America, where the word was recorded as "bee," perhaps by folk etymology from the dialectical English *been*. The word may have been influenced in its transcription by the insect, as bees are known for their ability to work together. William and May Morris (editors, *Morris Dictionary of Word and Phrase Origins*, New York: Harper and Row, 1977, 2nd. ed.) note that although the name seems an American invention, social gatherings where work for common or charitable purposes was done have been known in England since the Middle Ages. They also note the earlier American use of "bee" for spinning bouts. In fact, one of the earliest printed usages of "bee" was in the *Boston Gazette*, October 16, 1769: "Last Thursday about 20 young Ladies met at the house of Mr. L. on purpose for a Spinning Match (or what is called in the Country a Bee)." By 1809, Washington Irving was including the word in his stories: "Now were instituted quilting bees and husking bees and other rural assemblages" (*Knickerbocker Papers*). It is of interest to note that "bee" has been used for communal activities almost exclusively in reference to rural events; it was rarely used in connection with urban activities until well into the nineteenth century, when its usage was applied universally to quilting parties but never to male-dominated urban communal events.

5. A.D.P. Van Buren, *Pioneer Collections*, as quoted in Marsha MacDowell and Ruth D. Fitzgerald, eds., *Michigan Quilts: 150 Years of a Texile Tradition* (East Lansing, MI: Michigan State University Museum, 1987), p. 5. Sometimes these communal gatherings served a dual purpose; Ruth Henshaw Bascomb's journal notes her attendance at a quilting when, at the same time, the men of the family were holding a husking bee. As mentioned in Jonathan Holstein, *The Pieced Quilt: An American Design Tradition* (Greenwich, CT: The New York Graphic Society, 1973), p. 85.

6. Dr. J.G.M. Ramsey, *Annals of Old Tennessee* (1853), as quoted in Marie D. Webster, *Quilts: Their Story and How to Make Them* (New York: Doubleday, Page & Co., 1915), p. 152.

7. Dolores Hayden, *The Grand Revolution: A History of Feminist Designs for American Homes, Neighborhoods, and Cities* (Cambridge, MA: MIT Press, 1981), p. 79. See also Alice Morse Earle, *Home Life in Colonial Days* (1898; Stockbridge, MA: Berkshire Traveller Press, 1974), p. 417. Women would join forces on a small scale for "change-work"; two would do some chore such as making soap at one house, then a few days later repeat the work at the other's house. "Whang" was defined as a gathering of a few friendly women neighbors to assist in the "dismal task of annual house cleaning."

8. Jack Larkin, *The Reshaping of Everyday Life 1790–1840* (New York: Harper & Row Publishers, 1988), p. 298.

9. Nancy Grey Osterud, *Bonds of Community: The Lives of Farm Women in Nineteenth-Century New York* (Ithaca, NY: Cornell University Press, 1991), p. 232.

10. See, for example, Nancy F. Cott, *The Bonds of Womanhood: "Woman's Sphere" in New England, 1780–1835* (New Haven: Yale University Press, 1977).

11. Pat Ferrero, Elaine Hedges, and Julie Silber, *Hearts and Hands: The Influence of Women and Quilts on American Society* (San Francisco: Quilt Digest Press, 1987), p. 27.

12. Osterud, *Bonds of Community*, p. 299.

13. Glenna Matthews, *"Just a Housewife": The Rise and Fall of Domesticity in America* (New York: Oxford University Press, 1987), p. 222.

14. Rosemary O. Joyce, *A Woman's Place: The Life History of a Rural Ohio Grandmother* (Columbus: Ohio State University Press, 1983), p. 190.

MANY HANDS MAKE LIGHT WORK

1. Thomas Low Nichols, from Oxford, New Hampshire, 1815, as quoted in Elizabeth D. Garrett, *The Arts of Independence: The DAR Collection* (Washington, DC: Daughters of the American Revolution, 1985), p. 99.

2. Frances Trollope, *Domestic Manners of the Americans*, Donald Smalley, editor (New York: 1949 edition), p. 414.

3. As quoted in Julie Roy Jeffrey, *Frontier Women: The Trans-Mississippi West 1840-1880* (New York: Hill and Wang, 1979), p. 86.

4. "'Apple Bee' and 'Quilting Bee' in New York State in the 1830s as Described by Richard Weston, Edinburgh Bookseller," *The American Magazine*, Vol. 4, No. 1 (Spring-Summer 1988), p. 19. Weston noted that 38 men and 35 women attended this event. He also included a good description of how the quilting frame was set up: "A square frame was fastened together at the four corners, and suspended from the roof.... The lining of cotton was laced to the frame, several folds of cotton cadice being laid on it, above which was placed the upper covering, also laced to the frame, and around the frame itself a square of clap boards for seats to the ladies."

5. As quoted in Lynn A. Bonfield, "Diaries of New England Quilters Before 1860," *Uncoverings 1988*, Vol. 9, 1989, p. 184.

6. Mrs. Anna Foster, an early resident of Batavia, Genesee County, as quoted in Orasmus Turner, *The Pioneer History of the Holland Purchase*, 1849, p. 471.

7. Marie D. Webster, *Quilts: Their Story and How to Make Them* (New York: Doubleday, Page & Co., 1915), p. 156.

8. From a letter written by John Sutter, founder of New Helvetia (Sutter's Fort), as quoted in Sally Garoutte, "California's First Quilting Party," *Uncoverings 1981*, Vol. 2, 1982, p. 56. The quilting party was held by Sarah Armstrong Montgomery on January 29, 1846, and Sutter had given leave to the men who worked for him to attend the party.

9. Ruth E. Finley, *Old Patchwork Quilts and the Women Who Made Them* (Newton Centre, MA: Charles T. Branford Co., 1929, repr. 1970).

10. From Mary Wilkins Freeman, "A Quilting Bee in Our Village," *The People of Our Neighborhood* (Philadelphia: Curtis Publishing Company, 1898), as quoted in Dorothy Cozart, "Women and Their Quilts as Portrayed by Some American Authors," *Uncoverings 1981*, Vol. 2, 1982, p. 23.

11. For a good survey of quiltings and bees as portrayed in literature, see Cozart, "Women and Their Quilts as Portrayed by Some American Authors," pp. 19-33. See also Jeannette Lasansky, ed., *In the Heart of Pennsylvania: Nineteenth and Twentieth Century Quiltmaking Traditions* (Lewisburg, PA: Oral Traditions Project of the Union County Historical Society, 1985), for a number of poems and other literary references to bees and quilting.

12. "'Apple Bee' and 'Quilting Bee' in New York State," p. 20.

13. Martha Moore Ballard, November 10, 1790, as quoted in June Sprigg, *Domestick Beings* (New York: Alfred A. Knopf, 1984), p. 162.

14. Elias Nason, "A New England Village Quilting Party in Olden Times," *Granite Monthly*, 8, 1885, p. 235.

15. Harriet Beecher Stowe, "The Minister's Wooing," as quoted in Carrie A. Hall and Rose G. Kretsinger, *The Romance of the Patchwork Quilt in America* (New York: Bonanza Books, reprint of 1935 ed.), pp. 23, 26.

16. Mary Small Wagner, "The Patchwork Quilt," *The Designer*, May 1904, p. 69.

17. As quoted in Ricky Clark, ed., *Quilts in Community: Ohio's Traditions. Nineteenth and Twentieth Century Quilts, Quiltmakers, and Traditions* (Nashville, TN: Rutledge Hill Press, 1991), p. 108.

18. Nason, "A New England Village Quilting Party in Olden Times," p. 235.

19. From "Quilting at Miss Jones," *Godey's Lady's Book*, 1868, as quoted in Jonathan Holstein, *The Pieced Quilt: An American Design Tradition* (Greenwich, CT: The New York Graphic Society, 1973), p. 87.

20. Phebe Earle Gibbons, *Pennsylvania Dutch and Other Essays* (Philadelphia: J. B. Lippincott, 1874), p. 35.

21. As quoted in Bonfield, "Diaries of New England Quilters before 1860," p. 183.

22. Catherine Clinton, *The Plantation Mistress: Woman's World in the Old South* (New York: Pantheon Books, 1982), p. 26.

23. For several examples of slave-made quilts, see Cuesta Benberry, *Always There: The African-American Presence in American Quilts* (Louisville, KY: The Kentucky Quilt Project, Inc., 1992) and Gladys-Marie Fry, *Stitched from the Soul: Slave Quilts from the Ante-Bellum South* (New York: Dutton Studio Books, 1990).

24. As quoted in Fry, *Stitched from the Soul*, p. 74.

25. Ibid., p. 80.

26. Ibid., p. 77.

27. "'Apple Bee' and 'Quilting Bee' in New York State," pp. 15-18.

28. Nancy Callahan, "Helping the Peoples to Help Themselves," *Quilt Digest* 4 (1986), pp. 23-24. See also Benberry, *Always There*, p. 61.

29. Callahan, "Helping the Peoples to Help Themselves," p. 24.

30. Ibid., p. 26.

A FAMILY AFFAIR

1. Letter from Thomas Jefferson to his daughter Martha on March 28, 1787, as quoted in Gloria Seaman Allen, *First Flowerings: Early Virginia Quilts* (Washington, DC: DAR Museum, 1987), p. 9.

2. As quoted in Lynn A. Bonfield, "Diaries of New England Quilters Before 1860," *Uncoverings 1988*, Vol. 9, 1989, p. 189.

3. As quoted in Cuesta Benberry, *Always There: The African-American Presence in American Quilts* (Louisville, KY: The Kentucky Quilt Project, Inc., 1992), p. 60.

4. See diary entries for Elizabeth Porter Phelps, June 26, 1768, and October 5 and 26, 1788, as quoted in Bonfield, "Diaries of New England Quilters Before 1860," pp. 189, 191. Many of the references to quilting in Phelps's earliest diaries refer to quilting petticoats or coats rather than bed quilts, although some of the entries do specifically mention bed quilts. It should be remembered that until the mid-eighteenth century a major portion of a woman's time was spent in the production of cloth and clothing, and that quilting was most often confined to articles of apparel. It was not until somewhat later, when manufactured textiles began to be more easily available, that

bed quilting began to play a larger part in the everyday sewing life.

5. John Rice Irwin, *A People and Their Quilts* (Exton, PA: Schiffer Publishing Co., 1984).

6. As quoted in Allen, *First Flowerings: Early Virginia Quilts*, p. 9.

7. The Kentucky Quilt Project, *Kentucky Quilts 1800–1900* (Louisville, KY: The Kentucky Quilt Project, 1982), p. 49.

8. Nancy Grey Osterud, *Bonds of Community: The Lives of Farm Women in Nineteenth-Century New York* (Ithaca, NY: Cornell University Press, 1991), p. 12.

9. In a letter from Lucy Ambler, as quoted in Allen, *First Flowerings: Early Virginia Quilts*, p. 10. The Mrs. Amber referred to was Lucy's mother-in-law; Catherine and Elizabeth were her sisters-in-law.

10. From the diary of Ellen Birdseye Wheaton, as quoted in Mirra Bank, *Anonymous was a Woman* (New York: St. Martin's Press, 1979), p. 92.

11. From the journal of Mary Richardson Walker, as quoted in Bank, *Anonymous was a Woman*, p. 79.

12. From the journal of Ann Booth, as quoted in Julie Roy Jeffrey, *Frontier Women: The Trans-Mississippi West 1840–1880* (New York: Hill and Wang, 1979), p. 56. Henry was Ann Booth's husband.

13. See, for example, John Rice Irwin, *A People and Their Quilts*, and Patricia Cooper and Norma Bradley Buferd, *The Quilters: Women and Domestic Art—An Oral History* (New York: Doubleday, 1977; Anchor Press, 1978), p. 154. Irwin also noted that occasionally a woman would put out word "that they's having a quilting party on a certain night, and several neighborhood women would gather in.... They wouldn't come from too far away."

MATRIMONY MUST EVEN BE TRIED

1. Caroline Cowles Richards, *Village Life in America, 1852-1872, as told in the Diary of a School-Girl* (Williamstown, MA: Corner House Publishers, 1972; Henry Holt & Co., 1913).

2. Nancy Grey Osterud, *Bonds of Community: The Lives of Farm Women in Nineteenth-Century New York* (Ithaca, NY: Cornell University Press, 1991), p. 69.

3. Jessica F. Nicoll, "Signature Quilts and the Quaker Community 1840–1860," *Uncoverings 1986*, Vol. 7, 1987, p. 30.

4. See, for example, Dorothy Cozart, "Women and Their Quilts as Portrayed by Some American Authors," *Uncoverings 1981*, Vol. 2, 1982, pp. 19-33.

5. Lynn A. Bonfield, "Diaries of New England Quilters Before 1860," *Uncoverings 1988*, Vol. 9, 1989, pp. 171-197.

6. Mary Wilkins Freeman, "A Quilting Bee in Our Village," as quoted in Dorothy Cozart, "Women and Their Quilts as Portrayed by Some American Authors," *Uncoverings 1981*, Vol. 2, 1982, pp. 23-24. This story not only uses a bee for a mother to announce the engagement of her daughter but also highlights the importance of the engagement quilt by pointing out, through the medium of two shocked gossips, that new material had been bought to use in the quilt!

7. Dolores A. Hinson, *Quilting Manual* (New York: Dover Publications, Inc., reprint, 1980).

8. T.S. Arthur, "The Quilting Party," *Godey's Lady's Book*, Vol. 39, September, 1849, p. 185.

9. George Washington Harris, "Mrs. Yardley's Quilting," as quoted in Cozart, "Women and Their Quilts as Portrayed by Some American Authors," pp. 21-22.

10. Harriet Beecher Stowe, "The Minister's Wooing," (Boston: James R. Osgood and Co., 1875), pp, 287-297.

11. Patricia Cooper and Norma Bradley Buferd, *The Quilters: Women and Domestic Art* (New York: Anchor Press/ Doubleday, 1978), p. 68.

12. Richards, *Village Life in America, 1852-1872*, Friday, December 13, 1859, entry, p. 114.

13. From the Records of The Young Ladies Sewing Society of Canandaigua, 1861, as quoted in Shelly Zegart, "Old Maid, New Woman," *Quilt Digest 4*, 1986, p. 55.

14. Richards, *Village Life in America*, p. 114.

15. Zegart, "Old Maid, New Woman," p. 57.

16. Richards, *Village Life in America*, p. 49: "December 20, 1855.—Susan B. Anthony is in town and spoke in Bemis Hall this afternoon. She made a special request that all seminary [the Ontario Female Academy] girls should come to hear her as well as all the women and girls in town. She had a large audience and talked very plainly about our rights and how we ought to stand up for them.... She asked us all to come up and sign our names who would promise to do all in our power to bring about that glad day when equal rights should be the law of the land. A whole lot of us went up and signed the paper."

17. Lee Virginia Chamber-Schiller, *Liberty, A Better Husband* (New Haven: Yale University Press, 1984), p. 18.

18. *100th Anniversary Booklet of the First Congregational Church, Canandaigua, N.Y.*, as quoted in Zegart, "Old Maid, New Woman," p. 62.

19. William Rush Dunton, Jr., M.D., *Old Quilts* (Catonville, MD: self-published, 1946), pp. 76-77.

20. Finley, *Old Patchwork Quilts*, p. 192.

21. Karoline Patterson Bresenhan and Nancy O'Bryant Puentes, *Lone Stars: A Legacy of Texas Quilts, 1836–1936* (Austin: University of Texas Press, 1986), pp. 90-91.

FRIENDSHIP'S DUE

1. New York: Villard Books, 1991; p. 71.

2. Miss Florence Hartley, *Ladies Hand Book of Fancy and Ornamental Work* (Philadelphia, 1859), as quoted in Jacqueline M. Atkins and Phyllis A. Tepper, *New York Beauties: Quilts from the Empire State* (New York: Dutton Studio Books, 1992), p. 110.

3. Robert J. Schleck, *The Wilcox Quilts in Hawaii* (Kauai, Hawaii: Grove Farm Homestead and Waioli Mission House, 1986), p. 15.

4. Dena S. Katzenberg, *Baltimore Album Quilts* (Baltimore, MD: The Baltimore Museum of Art, 1981).

5. Frequently a pastor or another man was asked to do the signatures, especially if he were thought to be skilled in calligraphy and could offer an extra decorative touch to the names.

6. According to Barbara Brackman in *Clues in the Calico: A Guide to Identifying and Dating Antique Quilts* (McClean, VA: EMP Publications, Inc., 1989), Payson's Indelible Ink, which came on the market in 1834, was still considered at the end of the

century as among the best and most long-lasting ink for marking fabric (p. 118).

7. Katzenberg, *Baltimore Album Quilts*, p. 42. One might also view the elaborate floral motifs that appear in many album quilts as a fabric representation of the decorative drawings that embellish many autograph albums.

8. Jane Bentley Kolter, *Forget Me Not: A Gallery of Friendship and Album Quilts* (Pittstown, NJ: The Main Street Press, 1985), p. 9.

9. Ruth E. Finley, *Old Patchwork Quilts and the Women Who Made Them* (Newton Centre, MA: Charles T. Branford Co., 1970), p. 192.

10. Myron and Patsy Orlofsky, *Quilts in America* (New York: McGraw-Hill, 1974; rev. ed. Abbeville Press, 1992), pp. 252-53.

11. From the journal of Ann Booth, as quoted in Julie Roy Jeffrey, *Frontier Women: The Trans-Mississippi West 1840–1880* (New York: Hill and Wang, 1979), pp. 37, 56.

12. Jeffrey, *Frontier Women*, p. 56.

13. Lillian Schlissel, *Women's Diaries of the Westward Journey* (New York: Schocken Books, 1982), p. 30.

14. Eliza Marshall Gregson, as quoted in Sally Garoutte, "California's First Quilting Party," *Uncoverings 1981*, Vol. 2, 1982, p. 56. In this same article, Garoutte writes of Sarah Armstrong Montgomery, who organized the quilting party of the title to which eleven women came, many of whom had to travel thirty miles or more on horseback to get there. Many of these women, like Eliza Gregson, were the only women in their communities and welcomed the opportunity for female companionship, whatever the inconvenience and distance involved.

15. Linda Otto Lipsett, in her book *Remember Me: Women and Their Friendship Quilts* (San Francisco: Quilt Digest Press, 1985), has provided some excellent documentation on the meaning of Friendship quilts to their owners.

16. See, for example, Jessica F. Nicoll, "Signature Quilts and the Quaker Community 1840–1860," *Uncoverings 1986*, Vol. 7, 1987, pp. 27-37; and Jessica F. Nicoll, *Quilted for Friends: Delaware Valley Signature Quilts, 1840–1855* (Winterthur, DE: Henry Francis du Pont Winterthur Museum, 1986).

A SYMBOL OF RESPECT AND ADMIRATION

1. "The William Rush Dunton, Jr. Notebooks," Vol. VIII, uncatalogued collection, Baltimore Museum of Art, 1938, 128.

2. As quoted in Patricia Cooper and Norma Bradley Buferd, *The Quilters: Women and Domestic Art* (New York: Anchor Press/Doubleday, 1978), p. 89.

3. Dena S. Katzenberg, *Baltimore Album Quilts* (Baltimore, MD: The Baltimore Museum of Art, 1981).

4. From Rosella Frisbee's diary, 1861, as quoted in Joyce Ice and Linda Norris, *Quilted Together: Women, Quilts, and Communities* (Delhi, NY: Delaware County Historical Association, 1989), p. 6.

5. As quoted in Cooper and Buferd, *The Quilters: Women and Domestic Art*, pp. 89-90.

6. These latter two quilts are included in Cuesta Benberry, *Always There: The African-American Presence in American Quilts* (Louisville, KY: The Kentucky Quilt Project, Inc., 1992), pp. 58, 101, 102.

1. Julie Roy Jeffrey, *Frontier Women: The Trans-Mississippi West 1840-1880* (New York: Hill and Wang, 1979), p. 98.

2. As quoted in Dorothy Cozart, "A Century of Fundraising Quilts: 1860-1960," *Uncoverings 1985*, Vol. 6, 1986, p. 42.

3. "One Thousand Dollars for the Red Cross Can Be Raised on a Memorial Quilt," *The Modern Priscilla*, December 1917, p. 2.

4. Ricky Clark, "The Needlework of an American Lady: Social History in Quilts," in Jeannette Lasansky, ed., *In the Heart of Pennsylvania: Symposium Papers* (Lewisburg, PA: Oral Traditions Project of the Union County Historical Society, 1986), p. 72.

5. Miriam Gurko, *The Ladies of Seneca Falls: The Birth of the Woman's Rights Movement* (New York: Schocken Books, 1976), p. 24.

6. Jeffrey, *Frontier Women*, p. 87.

7. See Joella Vreeland, *The Southold Sisterhood—Sociables and Serious Business* (Southold, NY: Academy Printing Services, 1985), an interpretive journal based on the twenty-two hand-written volumes of minutes and treasurer's books of the Ladies Sewing Society of the First Universalist Church of Southold, New York in 1845.

8. Some early church leaders, John Wesley among them, encouraged women to form societies so that they would have an opportunity to gain some relief from their endless household tasks. The important social function that these groups could play, especially in more remote communities, has also been recognized by ministers' wives, some of whom have been instrumental in their formation. See, for example, Debra Ballard, "The Ladies Aid of Hope Lutheran Church," *Uncoverings 1989*, Vol. 10, 1990, pp. 69-79, in which a member tells how the reverend's wife organized a quilting group because "she thought that would be a nice thing to do for the women to get together 'cause the women didn't get out very often" (p. 70).

9. Jeffrey, *Frontier Women*, p. 86.

10. Dorothy Cozart notes that the earliest Signature quilts of this type may date from the 1850s and have been made in Pennsylvania. See Cozart, "The Role and Look of Fundraising Quilts 1850-1930," in Jeannette Lasansky, ed., *Pieced by Mother: Symposium Papers* (Lewisburg, PA: Oral Traditions Project of the Union County Historical Society, 1988), p. 87.

11. Jeannette Lasansky, ed., *Pieced by Mother: Over 100 Years of Quiltmaking Traditions* (Lewisburg, PA: Oral Traditions Project of the Union County Historical Society, 1987), p. 63.

12. Cozart, "The Role and Look of Fundraising Quilts 1850-1930," p. 93.

13. Ibid., p. 94.

14. Cozart, "A Century of Fundraising Quilts: 1860-1960," pp. 46–47. This article also provides an excellent look at the range of causes for which fundraising quilts were made, from missionary support to murder cases.

15. Florence Peto, *Historic Quilts* (New York: The American Historical Company, 1939), p. 37.

16. Cozart, "The Role and Look of Fundraising Quilts 1850-1930," p. 93.

17. Clark, "The Needlework of an American Lady," p. 71.

18. Ricky Clark, ed., *Quilts in Community: Ohio's Traditions*.

Nineteenth and Twentieth Century Quilts, Quiltmakers, and Traditions (Nashville, TN: Rutledge Hill Press, 1991), p. 136.

19. Ibid.

20. As quoted in Ballard, "The Ladies Aid of Hope Lutheran Church," p. 72.

PRICKING THE SOCIAL CONSCIENCE

1. From the dedication of the 1¼-mile-long banner made by Church Women United as their contribution for the Peace Ribbon, as quoted in Marianne Philbin, editor, *The Ribbon: A Celebration of Life* (Asheville, NC: Lark Books, 1985), p. 24.

2. Some believe that the collective consciousness engendered by participation in such groups set the stage for women's political activism later in the century. See, for example, Nancy F. Cott, *The Bonds of Womanhood: "Woman's Sphere" in New England, 1780–1835* (New Haven: Yale University Press, 1977), p. 193.

3. Ricky Clark, "The Needlework of an American Lady: Social History in Quilts," in Jeannette Lasansky, ed., *In the Heart of Pennsylvania: Symposium Papers* (Lewisburg, PA: Oral Traditions Project of the Union County Historical Society, 1986), p. 72.

4. Ricky Clark, *Quilts in Community: Ohio's Traditions. Nineteenth and Twentieth Century Quilts, Quiltmakers, and Traditions* (Nashville, TN: Rutledge Hill Press, 1991), p. 149.

5. Even though early male leaders of the temperance movement had proposed that women be permitted as equal members in the local temperance societies, they were largely ignored by the men who ran things. Women were allowed to form their own auxiliary societies, but they had no voice in the main society and could only endorse resolutions offered by male members. When Susan B. Anthony was prevented from speaking at the 1852 New York State Temperance Society Convention, she and Elizabeth Cady Stanton formed the Women's State Temperance Society, but they became powerless when men were admitted a year later and proceeded to fill all the important offices.

6. From Mother Thompson's reminiscences, *Hillsboro Crusade Sketches and Family Records*, 1906, as quoted in Clark, *Quilts in Community*, p. 149.

7. Temperance sentiment remained strong, especially in rural areas, for a number of years and a fundraiser quilt made in 1939 by a WCTU chapter in Tompkins County, New York, was registered during the New York Quilt Project (see Atkins and Tepper, *New York Beauties*, p. 89); twentieth-century examples from other parts of the country are also known.

8. Katharine Anthony, *Susan B. Anthony: Her Personal History and Her Era* (Garden City, NY: Doubleday & Company, Inc., 1954), p. 37.

9. The "ABC" in ABC Quilts was originally the acronym for AIDS Baby Crib (Quilts). It now stands for All Babies in Crisis Quilts.

THREE CHEERS FOR THE RED, WHITE, AND BLUE

1. Verses inscribed on a quilt mentioned in Ethel Alice Hurn, *Wisconsin Women in the War Between the States* (Madison, Wisconsin History Commission, 1911), as quoted in Virginia Gunn, "Quilts for Union Soldiers in the Civil War," *Uncoverings 1985*, Vol. 6, 1986, p. 111.

2. As quoted in Juliana Koenig, "The Public Quilt," *The Clarion*, Spring 1986, p. 68.

3. Wm. Howell Reed, as quoted in Jacqueline M. Atkins and Phyllis A. Tepper, *New York Beauties: Quilts from the Empire State* (New York: Dutton Studio Books, 1992), p. 27.

4. For more detailed information on the Sanitary Commission and Sanitary Fairs, see, for example, Wm. Howell Reed, *The Heroic Story of the U. S. Sanitary Commission, 1861–1865* (Boston: G. H. Ellis, n.d.) and James M. McPherson, *Battle Cry of Freedom: The Civil War Era* (New York: Oxford University Press, 1988).

5. Gunn, "Quilts for Union Soldiers in the Civil War," pp. 97, 112.

6. Henry W. Bellows, from "U.S. Sanitary Comm. Doc. No. 63—A Letter to the Women of the Northwest, Assembled at the Fair at Chicago, for the Benefit of the U.S. Sanitary Comm.," Documents of the U.S. Sanitary Comm., Vol. 11, pp. 3-4, as quoted in Gunn, "Quilts for Union Soldiers," p. 115.

7. Caroline Cowles Richards, *Village Life in America 1852–1872* (New York: Henry Holt & Co., 1913), pp. 132, 152, 205-206.

8. The Confederacy's Soldiers' Relief Society was established during the War, but a lack of coordination among the states precluded it from having the impact of the Sanitary Commission. See Dorothy Cozart, "The Role and Look of Fundraising Quilts 1850-1930," in Jeannette Lasansky, ed., *Pieced by Mother: Symposium Papers* (Lewisburg, PA: Oral Traditions Project of the Union County Historical Society, 1988), p. 88.

9. Laurel Horton, "South Carolina's Quilts and the Civil War," *Uncoverings 1985*, Vol. 6, 1986, p. 57.

10. Cuesta Benberry, "The 20th Century's First Great Quilt Revival," *Quilter's Newsletter*, October 1979.

11. Nancy J. Rowley, "Red Cross Quilts for the Great War," *Uncoverings 1982*, Vol. 3, 1983, p. 45.

12. See, for example, Pat Long, "Quiltmaking in the Richland, Pennsylvania, Church of the Brethren, 1914–1937," *Uncoverings 1988*, Vol. 9, 1989, pp. 73-83.

13. Joyce B. Peaden, "Donated Quilts Warmed Wartorn Europe," *Uncoverings 1988*, Vol. 9, 1989, pp. 29-44. According to Peaden, the Society made quilts both to teach members and to inspire recipients. Tops might be made individually, but were quilted in groups, usually in one or two sittings. Other church groups were equally active during World War II; see, for example, Debra Ballard, "The Ladies Aid of Hope Lutheran Church," *Uncoverings 1989*, Vol. 10, 1990, pp. 69-79.

14. Robert Bishop and Carter Houck, *All Flags Flying: American Patriotic Quilts as Expressions of Liberty* (New York: E.P. Dutton, 1986), p. 43.

15. Information on this quilt is courtesy of Joel Kopp, America Hurrah Antiques, NYC. Further research is still underway.

16. See, for example, Bishop and Houck, *All Flags Flying: American Patriotic Quilts as Expressions of Liberty.*

"I WILL REMEMBER THEE"

1. From Susan N. Burr's memorial quilt, as quoted in Gail

Andrews Treschel, "Mourning Quilts in America," *Uncoverings 1989*, Vol. 10, 1990, pp. 143-144.

2. As quoted in ibid., p. 140.

3. Daniel E. Sutherland, *The Expansion of Everyday Life 1860–1876* (New York: Harper and Row, 1989), p. 127. Sutherland further notes that less than ten percent of all Americans who reached the age of fifteen in the 1870s had both parents and all their siblings under age fifteen still living.

4. Martha V. Pike and Janice Gray Armstrong, eds., *A Time to Grieve: Expressions of Grief in Nineteenth Century America* (Stony Brook, NY: The Museums at Stony Brook, 1980), p. 19.

5. As quoted in Patricia Cooper and Norma Bradley Buferd, *The Quilters: Women and Domestic Art* (New York: Anchor Press/Doubleday, 1978), p. 49.

6. July 28, 1877, diary entry, as quoted in Nancy Grey Osterud, *Bonds of Community: The Lives of Farm Women in Nineteenth-Century New York* (Ithaca, NY: Cornell University Press, 1991), p. 121.

7. Treschel, "Mourning Quilts in America," p. 144.

8. Ibid., p. 151.

9. See, for example, Jessica F. Nicoll, "Signature Quilts and the Quaker Community 1840–1860," *Uncoverings 1986*, Vol. 7, 1987, pp. 27-37.

10. Treschel, "Mourning Quilts in America," p. 148.

11. Such a threat was childbirth that one woman, in the midst of her first pregnancy, told her sister that "I have made my will and divided off all my little things and don't mean to leave undone what I ought to do. Sometimes I think I must be very frivolous to not keep a steady eye on death and eternity all the time." (As quoted in Sutherland, *The Expansion of Everyday Life*, pp. 126-127.)

12. Ricky Clark, "Fragile Families: Quilts as Kinship Bonds," *Quilt Digest 5*, 1987, pp. 4-19.

13. "The Patchwork Quilt," *Lowell Offering*, December 1845, reprinted in Benita Eisler, editor, *The Lowell Offering: Writings of New England Mill Women (1840–1845)* (New York: Harper and Row, 1977), p. 154.

14. As quoted in Susan Roach, "The Kinship Quilt," in Rosan A. Jordan and Susan J. Kalcik, eds., *Women's Folklore, Women's Culture* (Philadelphia: University of Pennsylvania Press 1985), p. 59.

15. This quilt, a Log Cabin in the Barn Raising pattern, made by Rebecca Driggs Latta and her daughter Mary, used a red fabric in its center squares to signify the hearth of the log cabin that was symbolic of Lincoln's early life in that state. Indiana Quilt Registry Project, Inc., *Quilts of Indiana: Crossroads of Memories* (Bloomington, IN: Indiana University Press, 1991), p. 30.

16. Dena S. Katzenberg, *Baltimore Album Quilts* (Baltimore, MD: The Baltimore Museum of Art, 1981), pp. 51, 55.

17. Treschel, "Mourning Quilts in America," pp. 154-155.

THE MORE OF YOU THERE ARE

1. As quoted in Joyce Ice and Linda Norris, *Quilted Together: Women, Quilts, and Communities* (Delhi, NY: Delaware County Historical Association, 1989), p. 6.

2. As quoted in Mary Cross, "Reflections on an Oregon Quilt Contest," in Jeannette Lasansky, ed., *Bits and Pieces: Textile Traditions* (Lewisburg, PA: Oral Traditions Project of the Union County Historical Society, 1991), p. 108.

3. As quoted in Ice and Norris, *Quilted Together: Women, Quilts, and Communities*, p. 24.

4. As quoted in Kristin M. Langellier, "Contemporary Quiltmaking in Maine: Re-Fashioning Femininity," *Uncoverings 1990*, Vol. 11, 1991, p. 47.

5. Ibid., p. 45.

6. Cuesta Benberry, "White Perceptions of Blacks in Quilts and Related Media," *Uncoverings 1982*, Vol. 3, 1983, p. 68. It is also interesting to note that the central figure in the group of quilters that form the core of Whitney Otto's novel, *How to Make an American Quilt* (New York: Vintage Books, 1991), is a black woman.

7. Langellier, "Contemporary Quiltmaking in Maine," p. 46.

8. Cross, "Reflections on an Oregon Quilt Contest," p. 106.

9. Ibid., p. 104.

10. Debra Ballard, "The Ladies Aid of Hope Lutheran Church," *Uncoverings 1989*, Vol. 10, 1990, p. 69.

EPILOGUE

1. Cleve Jones, as quoted in Cindy Ruskin, *The Quilt: Stories from The NAMES Project* (New York: Pocket Books, 1988), p. 18.

2. Ibid., p. 18.

3. Ibid., p. 12.

Bibliography

Acker, Mary Rathbone. *My Dearest Anna: Letters of the Richmond Family 1836-1898*. Chicago: Adams Press, 1981.

Allen, Gloria Seaman. *First Flowerings: Early Virginia Quilts*. Washington, DC: DAR Museum, 1987.

An American Sampler: Folk Art from the Shelburne Museum. Washington, DC: National Gallery of Art, 1987.

Andrews, Ruth. *How to Know American Folk Art*. New York: E.P. Dutton, 1977.

Anthony, Katharine. *Susan B. Anthony, Her Personal History and Her Era*. Garden City, NY: Doubleday & Company, Inc., 1954.

"'Apple Bee' and 'Quilting Bee' in New York State in the 1830s as Described by Richard Weston, Edinburgh Bookseller." *The American Magazine*, Vol. 4, No. 1, Spring-Summer 1988, 13–22.

Arthur, T.S. "The Quilting Party." *Godey's Lady's Book*, Vol. 39, September 1849.

Atkins, Jacqueline M. and Phyllis A. Tepper. *New York Beauties: Quilts of the Empire State*. New York: Dutton Studio Books in association with the Museum of American Folk Art, 1992.

Ballard, Debra. "The Ladies Aid of Hope Lutheran Church," *Uncoverings 1989*, Vol. 10, 1990, 69–79.

Bank, Mirra. *Anonymous was a Woman*. New York: St. Martin's Press, 1979.

Benberry, Cuesta. *Always There: The African-American Presence in American Quilts*. Louisville, KY: The Kentucky Quilt Project, Inc., 1992.

————. "The Twentieth Century's First Great Quilt Revival." *Quilter's Newsletter*, October 1989.

————. "White Perceptions of Blacks in Quilts and Related Media." *Uncoverings 1982*, Vol. 3, 1983, 59–74.

Bishop, Robert. *New Discoveries in American Quilts*. New York: E.P. Dutton & Co., 1975.

————, and Carter Houck. *All Flags Flying: American Patriotic Quilts as Expressions of Liberty*. New York: E.P. Dutton in association with the Museum of American Folk Art, 1986.

————, William Secord, and Judith Reiter Weissman. *Quilts, Coverlets, Rugs, and Samplers*. New York: Alfred A. Knopf, 1982.

Bonfield, Lynn A. "Diaries of New England Quilters Before 1860." *Uncoverings 1988*, Vol. 9, 1989, 171–197.

————. "The Production of Cloth, Clothing, and Quilts in 19th Century New England Homes." *Uncoverings 1981*, Vol. 2, 1982, 77–96.

Boylan, Ann M. "Women in Groups: An Analysis of Women's Benevolent Organizations in New York and Boston, 1797–1840." *Journal of American History* 71, No. 3, December 1984, 497–523.

Brackman, Barbara. *Clues in the Calico: A Guide to Identifying and Dating Antique Quilts*. McLean, VA: EMP Publications, Inc., 1989.

————. "Memories: Looking Back at Five Years of Quilting Events." *Quilters' Newsletter Magazine*, September 1989, 32–34, 51.

————. "Signature Quilts: Nineteenth Century Trends." *Uncoverings 1989*, Vol. 10, 1990, 25–37.

Bresenhan, Karoline Patterson, and Nancy O'Bryant Puentes. *Lone Stars: A Legacy of Texas Quilts, 1836–1936*. Austin, TX: University of Texas Press, 1986.

Callahan, Nancy. "Helping the People to Help Themselves." *Quilt Digest 4*, 1986, 20–29.

Chamber-Schiller, Lee Virginia. *Liberty: A Better Husband*. New Haven, CT: Yale University Press, 1984.

Christopherson, Katy, commentator. *The Political and Campaign Quilt*. Frankfort, KY: The Kentucky Heritage Quilt Society and The Kentucky Historical Society, 1984.

Clark, Ricky. "Fragile Families: Quilts as Kinship Bonds." *Quilt Digest 5*, 1987, 4–19.

_____. "Mid 19th Century Album and Friendship Quilts 1860–1920," in, Jeannette Lasansky, ed. *Pieced by Mother: Symposium Papers.* Lewisburg, PA: Oral Traditions Project of the Union County Historical Society, 1988, 77–85.

_____. "The Needlework of an American Lady: Social History in Quilts," 65–77. In Jeannette Lasansky, ed., *In the Heart of Pennsylvania: Symposium Papers.* Lewisburg, PA: Oral Traditions Project of the Union County Historical Society, 1986.

_____, ed. *Quilts in Community: Ohio's Traditions. Nineteenth and Twentieth Century Quilts, Quiltmakers, and Traditions.* Nashville, TN: Rutledge Hill Press, 1991.

Clinton, Catherine. *The Plantation Mistress: Woman's World in the Old South.* New York: Pantheon Books, 1982.

Cooper, Patricia and Norma Bradley Buferd. *The Quilters: Women and Domestic Art.* New York: Doubleday, 1977.

Cott, Nancy F. *The Bonds of Womanhood: "Woman's Sphere" in New England 1780–1835.* New Haven, CT: Yale University Press, 1977.

Cozart, Dorothy. "A Century of Fundraising Quilts, 1860–1960," *Uncoverings 1985,* Vol. 6, 1986.

_____. "The Role and Look of Fundraising Quilts 1850–1930," in Jeannette Lasansky, ed. *Pieced by Mother: Symposium Papers.* Lewisburg, PA: Oral Traditions Project of the Union County Historical Society, 1988, 86–95.

_____. "Women and Their Quilts as Portrayed by Some American Authors," *Uncoverings 1981,* Vol. 2, 1982, 19–33.

Cross, Mary. "Reflections on an Oregon Quilt Contest." In Jeannette Lasansky, *Bits and Pieces: Textile Traditions.* Lewisburg, PA: Oral Traditions Project of the Union County Historical Society, 1991, 101–109.

Dewhurst, C. Kurt, Betty MacDowell, and Marsha MacDowell. *Artists in Aprons: Folk Art by American Women.* New York: E.P. Dutton in association with the Museum of American Folk Art, 1979.

_____. *Religious Folk Art in America: Reflections of Faith.* New York: E.P. Dutton in association with the Museum of American Folk Art, 1983.

Dow, George Francis. *Domestic Life in New England in the Seventeenth Century.* New York: Benjamin Bloom, Inc., 1972.

_____. "The Patchwork Quilt and Some Other Quilts." *Old-Time New England,* Vol. XVII, April 1927, No. 4, 157–173.

Dunton, William Rush, Jr. M.D. *Old Quilts.* Catonville, MD: self-published, 1946.

_____. "The William Rush Dunton Jr. Notebooks." Vol. VIII, 128. Uncatalogued Collection, Baltimore Museum of Art, 1938.

Earle, Alice Morse. *Home Life in Colonial Days.* 1898; Stockbridge, MA: Berkshire Traveller Press, 1974.

Eisler, Benita, editor. *The Lowell Offering: Writings of New England Mill Women (1840–1845).* New York: Harper and Row, 1977.

Ferrero, Pat, Elaine Hedges, and Julie Silber. *Hearts and Hands: The Influence of Women and Quilts in American Society.* San Francisco: Quilt Digest Press, 1987.

Finley, Ruth E. *Old Patchwork Quilts and the Women Who Made Them.* Newton Centre, MA: Charles T. Branford Co., 1929, repr. 1970.

Fox, Sandi. *Wrapped in Glory: Figurative Quilts and Bedcovers 1700–1900.* New York: Thames and Hudson and the Los Angeles County Museum of Art, 1990.

Friedlich, Karla. "Quilts of Conscience." *The Clarion,* Vol. 16, No. 1, Spring 1991, 47–54.

Fry, Gladys-Marie. *Stitched from the Soul: Slave Quilts from the Ante-Bellum South.* New York: Dutton Studio Books in association with the Museum of American Folk Art, 1990.

Furnas, J. C. *The Americans: A Social History 1587–1914.* New York: Capricorn Books, 1971.

Garoutte, Sally. "California's First Quilting Party." *Uncoverings 1981,* Vol. 2, 1982, 53–62.

_____. "Early Colonial Quilts in a Bedding Context." *Uncoverings 1980,* Vol. 1, 1981, 18–27.

Garrett, Elizabeth D. *The Arts of Independence: The DAR Collection.* Washington, DC: Daughters of the American Revolution, 1985.

Gibbons, Phebe Earle. *Pennsylvania Dutch and Other Essays.* Philadelphia: J.B. Lippincott, 1872, 33–35, particularly.

Gunn, Virginia. "Quilts for Union Soldiers in the Civil War." *Uncoverings 1985,* Vol. 6, 1986, 95–121.

Gurko, Miriam. *The Ladies of Seneca Falls: The Birth of the Woman's Rights Movement.* New York: Schocken Books, 1976.

Gutcheon, Jeffrey. "Not for Shopkeepers Only." *Quilter's Newsletter Magazine,* No. 163, June 1984, 26–27.

Haders, Phyllis. *Sunshine & Shadow: The Amish and Their Quilts.* Pittstown, NJ: The Main Street Press, 1984.

Hall, Carrie A. and Kretsinger, Rose G. *The Romance of the Patchwork Quilt in America.* New York: Bonanza Books, reprint of 1935 edition.

Hall, Eliza Calvert. *Aunt Jane in Kentucky.* Boston: Little, Brown & Co., 1908.

Hayden, Dolores. *The Grand Revolution: A History of Feminist Designs for American Homes, Neighborhoods, and Cities.* Cambridge, MA: MIT Press, 1981

Herr, Patricia T. "All in Modesty and Plainness." *Quilt Digest 3,* 1985.

————. "Quaker Quilts and Their Makers." In Jeannette Lasansky, ed. *Pieced by Mother: Symposium Papers.* Lewisburg, PA: Oral Traditions Project of the Union County Historical Society, 1988, 12–21.

Hinson, Dolores A. *Quilting Manual.* New York: Dover Publications, Inc., reprint, 1980.

Hoffman, Victoria. *Quilts: A Window to the Past.* North Andover, MA: Museum of American Textile History, 1991.

Holstein, Jonathan. *The Pieced Quilt: An American Design Tradition.* Greenwich, CT: The New York Graphic Society, 1973.

————. "Collecting Quilt Data." *Quilt Digest,* 1983, 62–68.

Horton, Laurel. "Quiltmaking Traditions in South Carolina." *Uncoverings 1984,* Vol. 5, 1985, 55–69.

————. "South Carolina Quilts and the Civil War." *Uncoverings 1985,* Vol. 6, 1986, 53–69.

Ice, Joyce and Linda Norris. *Quilted Together: Women, Quilts, and Communities.* Delhi, NY: Delaware County Historical Association, 1989.

Indiana Quilt Registry Project, Inc. *Quilts of Indiana: Crossroads of Memories.* Bloomington, IN: Indiana University Press, 1991.

Irwin, John Rice. *A People and Their Quilts.* Exton, PA: Schiffer Publishing Co., 1984.

Jeffrey, Julie Roy. *Frontier Women: The Trans-Mississippi West 1840–1880.* New York: Hill and Wang, 1979.

Jensen, Joan M. *Loosening the Bonds: Mid-Atlantic Farm Women 1750–1850.* New Haven, CT: Yale University Press, 1986.

———— and Sue Davidson, *A Needle, A Bobbin, A Strike.* Philadelphia: Temple University Press, 1984.

Johnson, Geraldine N. "More for Warmth Than for Looks: Quilts of the Blue Ridge Mountains," in Jeannette Lasansky, ed. *Pieced by Mother: Symposium Papers.* Lewisburg, PA: Oral Traditions Project of the Union County Historical Society, 1988, 46–59.

Joyce, Rosemary O. *A Woman's Place: The Life History of a Rural Ohio Grandmother.* Columbus: Ohio State University Press, 1983.

Katzenberg, Dena S. *Baltimore Album Quilts.* Baltimore, MD: The Baltimore Museum of Art, 1981.

Kentucky Quilt Project, The. *Kentucky Quilts 1800–1900.* Louisville, KY: The Kentucky Quilt Project, 1982.

Klimaszewski, Cathy Rosa. *Made to Remember: American Commemorative Quilts.* Ithaca, NY: Herbert F. Johnson Museum of Art, Cornell University, 1991

Koenig, Juliana. "The Public Quilt." *The Clarion,* Spring/Summer 1986, 66–73.

Kolter, Jane Bentley. *Forget Me Not: A Gallery of Friendship and Album Quilts.* Pittstown, NJ: The Main Street Press, 1985.

Langellier, Kristin M. "Contemporary Quiltmaking in Maine: Re-Fashioning Femininity." *Uncoverings 1990,* Vol. 11, 1991, 29–55.

Larkin, Jack. *The Reshaping of Everyday Life 1790–1840.* New York: Harper and Row, 1988.

Lasansky, Jeannette. *Bits and Pieces: Textile Traditions.* Lewisburg, PA: Oral Traditions Project of the Union County Historical Society, 1991.

————, ed. *In the Heart of Pennsylvania: 19th and 20th Century Quiltmaking Traditions.* Lewisburg, PA: Oral Traditions Project of the Union County Historical Society, 1985.

————, ed. *In the Heart of Pennsylvania: Symposium Papers.* Lewisburg, PA: Oral Traditions Project of the Union County Historical Society, 1986.

————, ed. *Pieced by Mother: Over 100 Years of Quiltmaking Traditions.* Lewisburg, PA: Oral Traditions Project, 1987.

————, ed. *Pieced by Mother: Symposium Papers.* Lewisburg, PA: Oral Traditions Project of the Union County Historical Society, 1988.

————. "The Colonial Revival and Quilts 1864–1976," in Jeannette Lasansky, ed. *Pieced by Mother: Symposium Papers.* Lewisburg, PA: Oral Traditions Project of the Union County Historical Society, 1988, 96–105.

Laverty, Paula. "Many Hands: The Story of an Album Quilt." *Folk Art,* Vol. 18, No. 1, Spring 1993, 52–57.

Lipsett, Linda Otto. *Remember Me: Women and Their Friendship Quilts.* San Francisco: Quilt Digest Press, 1985.

Long, Pat. "Quiltmaking in the Richland, Pennsylvania, Church of the Brethren, 1914–1937." *Uncoverings 1988,* Vol. 9, 1989, 73–83.

Lyman, Darryl. *The Animal Things We Say.* Middle Village, NY: Jonathan David Publishers, Inc., 1983.

MacDowell, Marsha and Ruth D. Fitzgerald, eds. *Michigan Quilts: 150 Years of a Textile Tradition.* East Lansing, MI: Michigan State University Museum, 1987.

McPherson, James M. *Battle Cry of Freedom: The Civil War Era.* New York: Oxford University Press, 1988.

Mainardi, Patricia. "Quilt Survivals and Revivals." *Arts Magazine,* May 1988, 49–53.

Matthews, Glenna. *"Just a Housewife": The Rise and Fall of Domesticity in America.* New York: Oxford University Press, 1987.

Melder, Keith. "Political Textiles in American History." *Fiberarts Magazine,* Vol. 17, No. 1, Summer 1990, 29-31.

Meyer, Suellen. "Early Influences of the Sewing Machine and Visible Machine Stitching on Nineteenth-Century Quilts." *Uncoverings 1989,* Vol. 10, 1990, 38-53.

Moore's Rural New-Yorker, September 23, 1854.

Moore's Rural New-Yorker, "Sewing Machines for the Farmer's Family," January 2, 1858.

Moore's Rural New-Yorker, "What a Farmer's Girl Should Know," January 31, 1863.

Morris, William and May, editors. *Morris Dictionary of Word and Phrase Origins.* New York: Harper and Row, 1977, 2nd. ed.

Museum of American Folk Art. *Expressions of a New Spirit.* New York: Museum of American Folk Art, 1989.

Nadelstern, Paula and LynNell Hancock. *Quilting Together: How to Organize, Design, and Make Group Quilts.* New York: Crown Publishers, 1988.

Nason, Elias. "A New England Village Quilting Party in the Olden Times." *The Granite Monthly,* Vol. 8, 1885, 235-239.

Nicoll, Jessica F. "Signature Quilts and the Quaker Community 1840-1860." *Uncoverings 1986,* Vol. 7, 1987, 27-37.

_____. *Quilted for Friends: Delaware Valley Signature Quilts, 1840-1855.* Winterthur, DE: Henry Francis du Pont Winterthur Museum, 1986.

Orlofsky, Patsy and Myron. *Quilts in America.* New York: McGraw-Hill, 1974; Abbeville Press, 1992.

Osterud, Nancy Grey. *Bonds of Community: The Lives of Farm Women in Nineteenth-Century New York.* Ithaca, NY: Cornell University Press, 1991.

Otto, Whitney. *How to Make an American Quilt.* New York: Vintage Books, 1991.

Oxford English Dictionary. Oxford: Clarendon Press, 1989, 2nd ed.

Peaden, Joyce B. "Donated Quilts Warmed Wartorn Europe." *Uncoverings 1988,* Vol. 9, 1989, 29-44.

Peto, Florence. *Historic Quilts.* New York: The American Historical Company, 1939.

Philbin, Marianne. *The Ribbon: A Celebration of Life.* Asheville, NC: Lark Books, 1985.

Pike, Martha V. and Janice Gray Armstrong, eds. *A Time to Grieve: Expressions of Grief in Nineteenth Century America.* Stony Brook, NY: The Museums at Stony Brook, 1980.

Ramsey, Bets. "Recollections of Childhood Recorded in a Tennessee Quilt." *Uncoverings 1983,* Vol. 4, 1984, 25-37.

_____ and Merikay Waldvogel. *The Quilts of Tennessee: Images of Domestic Life Prior to 1930.* Nashville, TN: Rutledge Hill Press, 1986.

Ramsey, J. G. M. *The Annals of Tennessee.* Charleston, SC: 1853.

Rawick, George P. *The American Slave: A Composite Autobiography.* Westport, CT: Greenwood, 1972.

Reed, Wm. Howell. *The Heroic Story of the U.S. Sanitary Commission, 1861-1865.* Boston: G.H. Ellis, n.d.

Richards, Caroline Cowles. *Village Life in America, 1852-1872, as told in the Diary of a Schoolgirl.* Williamstown, MA: Corner House Publishers, 1972, and New York: Henry Holt & Co., 1913.

Roach, Susan. "The Kinship Quilt: An Ethnographic Semiotic Analysis of a Quilting Bee," in Rosan A. Jordan and Susan J. Kalcik, eds. *Women's Folklore, Women's Culture.* Philadelphia: University of Pennsylvania Press, 1985.

Rowley, Nancy J. "Red Cross Quilts for the Great War." *Uncoverings 1982,* Vol. 3, 1983, 43-51.

Ruskin, Cindy. *The Quilt: Stories from the NAMES Project.* New York: Pocket Books, 1988.

Safford, Carleton L. and Robert Bishop. *America's Quilts and Coverlets.* New York: E. P. Dutton & Co., 1972.

Salahub, Jennifer E. "Swatches: Quilts—The Fabric of Society." *Fiberarts,* Summer 1990, 22-23.

Schleck, Robert J. *The Wilcox Quilts in Hawaii.* Kauai, Hawaii: Grove Farm Homestead and Waioli Mission house, 1986.

Schlissel, Lillian. *Women's Diaries of the Westward Journey.* New York: Schocken Books, 1982.

Schwoefferman, Catherine. *Threaded Memories: A Family Quilt Collection.* Exhibition Catalogue. Binghamton, NY: Roberson Center for the Arts and Sciences, 1984.

Scott, Anne Prior. *The Southern Lady: From Pedestal to Politics 1830-1930.* Chicago: University of Chicago Press, 1970.

Sienkiewicz, Elly. "Friendship's Offering," *Quilter's Newsletter Magazine,* May 1989, 32-33.

Sprigg, June. *Domestick Beings.* New York: Alfred A. Knopf, 1984.

Spruill, Julia Cherry. *Women in the Southern Colonies.* New York: W.W. Norton, 1972 (reprint of 1938 edition).

Strasser, Susan. *Never Done: A History of American Housework*. New York: Pantheon, 1982.

Stratton, Johanna L. *Pioneer Women: Voices from the Kansas Frontier*. New York: Simon and Schuster, 1981.

Stowe, Harriet Beecher. *The Minister's Wooing*. Boston: James R. Osgood and Co., 1875.

Sutherland, Daniel E. *The Expansion of Everyday Life 1860–1876*. New York: Harper and Row, Publishers, 1989.

Swan, Susan Barrows. *Plain and Fancy: American Women and Their Needlework 1700–1850*. New York: Holt, Rinehart and Winston, 1977.

————. "Quilting Within Women's Repertoire." In Jeannette Lasansky, ed., *In the Heart of Pennsylvania: Symposium Papers*. Lewisburg, PA: Oral Traditions Project of the Union County Historical Society, 1987, 8–15.

Townsend, Louise O. "What Was New & News in Quilting." *Quilter's Newsletter Magazine*, 15th Anniversary issue, 1984, 8–19.

Travis, Kathryne Hall. "Quilts of the Ozarks." *Southwest Review*, Vol. 1, January 1930.

Treschel, Gail Andrews. "Mourning Quilts in America." *Uncoverings 1989*, Vol. 10, 1990, 143–144.

Trollope, Frances. *Domestic Manners of the Americans*. Donald Smalley, editor. New York: 1949.

Turner, Orasmus. *The Pioneer History of the Holland Purchase*. New York, 1849.

Underwood, Francis. *Quabbin: The Story of a Small Town with Outlooks on Puritan Life*. Boston and London, 1893; reprinted Boston: Northeastern University Press, 1987.

Van Buren, A.D.P. "Raisings and Bees Among Early Settlers," *Pioneer Recollections, Report of the Pioneer Society of the State of Michigan*, Vol. V. Lansing, MI: W.S. George and Company, 1883, 296; see also "The Frolics of 45 Years Ago," 305.

Vreeland, Joella. *The Southold Sisterhood—Sociables and Serious Business*. Southold, NY: Academy Printing Services, 1985.

Wagner, Mary Small. "The Patchwork Quilt." *The Designer*. May 1904, 69.

Waldvogel, Merikay. *Soft Covers for Hard Times*. Nashville, TN: Rutledge Hill Press, 1990.

Webster, Marie D. *Quilts: Their Story and How to Make Them*. New York: Doubleday, Page & Co., 1915.

Weidlich, Lorre Marie. "Quilting Transformed: An Anthropological Approach to the Quilt Revival." Ph.D. Dissertation, University of Texas at Austin, 1986.

Zegart, Shelly. "Old Maid, New Woman." *Quilt Digest 4*, 1986, 54–65.

Index

INDEX TO QUILT PATTERNS
AND TYPES